The
'REJOICE
AND SING'
TOUR BOOK

ISBN 0 85346 146 5

Published by the United Reformed Church,
86 Tavistock Place, London WC1H 9RT

First Published 1995
© 1995 David Jenkins

Printed by Healeys, Ipswich

Contents

Preface

The acquiring of a new mainline hymnbook is an historic step for any congregation to take. It's a risk. And it's a major financial investment (though my experience leads me to believe that the money is found more painlessly than is at first feared!). More important, the decision is going to influence the life and worship of the congregation for a long time to come. It will shape the language, the beliefs, the hopes, the feelings of individuals and of the community. It will make people angry and it will make them delighted. Indeed, we could go so far as to say that this is one of the most formative moments which a congregation faces perhaps only once in a generation.

So that is why this book is rolling off the press. If you have purchased 'Rejoice and Sing' (or are about to!) I want you to make the most of this opportunity. This first hymn book of the United Reformed Church has been greeted with considerable warmth and enthusiasm not only within the denomination but by our ecumenical and international partners. It is far from perfect and the compilers are the first people to acknowledge the book's shortcomings. Yet it is an excellent resource not only for hymn and psalm singing but for public worship and private devotion. It will be sad if we fail to use it to its maximum.

I have built up the book on the lines of a holiday tour book! Not only does this provide a user-friendly framework, it opens doors for a positive exploration. For instance, if you go to Minorca for the first time, you can stay in your hotel and only venture as far as the beach. If you do this, you cannot really say you have been to Minorca! You've only been to a hotel and a beach! A tour book helps you to go further: to venture into new and surprising areas; to visit historical sites and to meet those who live on the island. Through the tour book you can make the most of what is on offer and be able to share your good and not-so-good discoveries with your friends. However, the analogy falls down at one crucial point. Moving on to '*Rejoice and Sing*' as a congregation is not a temporary break allowing you to 'return to normal after the holidays!' It is a decisive and irreversible step! All the more need, therefore, to make sure that you are immersing yourselves fully in the possibilities and dangers of the new experience! I hope this little book is a help.

I am grateful for the luxury of a Sabbatical to put this booklet together. What a privilege to work on a project which is a source of delight! I am also most grateful to a number of colleagues on the Hymnbook committees. David Thompson, Caryl Micklem, Caroline Brock, Brenda Stephenson, David Goodall and Paul Bateman have provided many pearls of wisdom. Stimulating conversations with others including Ray Adams, John Marsh and Stephen Thornton have given me encouragement. Margaret Urqhart (Durham) and Richard Hill (York Minster) have also given me valuable insights from their musical experience.

A fascinating visit to Dallas, Texas allowed me to tap the minds of leading musicians and hymnologists among whom were Hal Hopson, Kenneth Hart, Michael Hawn and Mary Oyer. My deep thanks go to the staff at the Choristers Guild who helped organise my itinerary and to my hosts, Don and Martha Fox for the warmth of their welcome.

A further visit to Santa Rosa, California enabled me also to be inspired by John Burke and Helen and John Kemp.

Most of these friends have much greater musical skills than I and I hope I have not let them down in what I have written.

Finally, my deepest appreciation goes to my wife, Margie, who not only puts up with my long absences whilst immersed in researching and writing but who has also frequently offered wise advice on the contents and script.

David Jenkins

Introduction

reparing for the Journey

Well, have you got the tickets? Got the traveller's cheques? Got the passports? Got the camera? Got your swimsuit? Got the Insurance sorted out? And don't forget the Tour Book!

So many things to remember! Any holiday needs considerable preparation. If it is to a new and exciting place, then you can't just take off without any planning! It is worth putting some time to get in the right frame of mind.

Making the most of *'Rejoice and Sing'* is also going to involve us in some preparation, and, dare we say it, some grafting! We can't expect to jump into a new hymn book and start from cold.

What, then, should be our starting point?

1. BEGIN WITH THE WORDS

If we ask: 'Where did the Hymnbook committee make their beginning?' The answer is: 'They began with the words'.

Now that may or may not surprise you. Certainly the tunes are extremely important, but we cannot approach a new hymnbook on whether or not our favourite tunes are set to particular hymns. A Hymnbook stands or falls on the quality of its words. So the first task is to get to know the words. When the Australian ecumenical hymn book *'With One Voice'* was published the 'Companion' (background) book had a three sections outlining the 'obligations' to ministers, organists, choirs and congregations. The first sentence in each of these sections was identical. It read: 'The first obligation of the leaders of services (organists...congregations) when the use of a new hymnal is begun is to read through the contents of the book including the preface.'

Now there's a challenge! Even if you don't read it all at once why not make a point of reading the hymns from a particular section or season at a particular time of year. One of the more frequent comments about *'Rejoice and Sing'* is that of approval for the words. Worshippers have even been heard to ask: 'Can I take the book home this week to read on my own?' That means the words are touching people's lives, their hopes, their pain, their dreams, their questions, their deepest experience. That makes a good hymn book!

The best hymn texts are not doggerel but thoughtful and beautiful poetry. They are words which will last; words which make you think; words which touch the depths of our need; words which challenge us and stretch us in our discipleship.

Richard Hill, who leads the choristers at York Minster, is insistent that singers cannot sing until the words have become part of them. 'They have to know what the words mean and they must become passionate about the message they convey. The words must get inside them!' That's very Biblical! The 'Word' must become flesh. It must be eaten (Ezekiel) and become part of us.

By starting with the words we are also beginning to discover how the book can be used. It can be used in worship and in private devotion without its music. As we dig deeper and explore further you will find all sorts of textual material which can be used for the value of the words alone. (See Tour 8: 'Words Only')

| 2. | **THINK ABOUT THE MUSIC** |

If we start with the words then we will realise that the aim of the music is to help the words come to life. Great care needs to be given in both the choice of tunes and the way in which the music is played. The compilers of *'Rejoice and Sing'* have tried to choose hymn tunes which fit the content and mood of the hymn texts. The most quoted (and controversial!) example of this concerns the well-known favourite 'And can it be...' The popularity of the tune *Sagina* has made many musicians squirm (not only Erik Routley, but many Methodist writers as well!) because Charles Wesley's words need not a fortissimo (ie. multo belto!)

rendering but a more sensitive and reflective setting. Not surprisingly *'Rejoice and Sing'* (No.366) prefers *'Abingdon'*.

Most contemporary hymn books do not insert the 'dynamics' (showing which verses or parts of verses should be loud and soft). Next Sunday try a little experiment before the service. Read through the hymns which have been chosen and think about the words. Which verses should be loud and which soft? Where is the climax of the hymn? You will be doing something the organist or music leader should also have done beforehand.

If we are to bring out the meaning and power of the words in our hymns we also need to think about how best to accompany each hymn. We have got into the habit of accompanying every hymn with an organ or piano, with the congregation singing all the verses. We've also become accustomed to standing for every hymn! Some verses may well suit a solo voice (eg. verses 3 & 4 of No. 474: 'Brother, sister, let me serve you'.) Similarly the excellent tune 'Out Skerries' (No.200 second tune) is suited more to piano and guitar (nb. composer Paul Bateman says it goes very well to organ and piano together!) The use of alternative instruments is growing in churches.

One thing is clear. You cannot settle down comfortably with *'Rejoice and Sing'* if you keep changing the tunes. Some churches have made a policy decision to sing the set tunes. That is very wise. The compilers have not always got it right, but they do have particular reasons for choosing the tunes which are printed. To return to our holiday analogy. We mustn't carry too much old baggage with us from 'back home'. It's like bringing wine from England to Spain. We must start to drink what is on offer in our new surroundings.

The need for a close partnership between the leader of worship and the organist or music-leader is absolutely essential. If we are going to make the most of *'Rejoice and Sing'* then all those responsible will have to plan further ahead than many do at present. Organists who complain at ministers 'throwing' a list of hymns at them five minutes before the service have a right to feel sorely aggrieved!

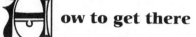

ow to get there

People going on holiday come from all places and travel by many varied means. They will come from various national backgrounds and will have a multitude of differing expectations.

It is not dissimilar in regard to our approach to a new hymn book. The new book must appeal to all sorts of congregations and individuals with tastes and backgrounds startlingly different. Churches in the United Reformed Church will have used all sorts of past hymnbooks. *Congregational Praise* and *Church Hymnary* (Third Edition) will have been the most common. But there will also have been *Revised Church Hymnary*, *Christian Hymnary*, and even the odd *Congregational Hymnary* in evidence. Then there is *Mission Praise* (1 and 2) and *Songs of Fellowship* which many churches have purchased in recent years. Methodist/United Reformed Churches will have been familiar with *Hymns and Psalms*. Churches which acquired *New Church Praise* (1972) will have a headstart with '*Rejoice and Sing*' because nearly half of those hymns have come through into the new publication (though beware! Some words and tunes have been altered!)

The compilers of '*Rejoice and Sing*' were aware of all these traditions. They were also aware that we have been experiencing a remarkable century of creative hymn-writing. The world church has been enriched by the skills and gifts of musicians and poets. The Holy Spirit is always busy! The world church is singing with energy and enthusiasm!

So much for where we come from. We reach our destination by many means. The decision to purchase '*Rejoice and Sing*' is still being made in a number of United Reformed Churches. Evidence from around the country supports the view that finance is not as big a hurdle as was feared. There have been many stories of personal gifts and legacies which have been generous and unexpected. It is wise to consider plastic covers to protect the books and thus give them a longer life. Available is the Full Music Edition which contains all the indexes; the melody edition (which has only an index of 'first lines'), and a large print words only edition. A Braille edition is also now available.

At the time of going to press, Oxford University Press still have their reduced offer for 'first time buyers'. This has proved very helpful for many congregations.

The Introductory Tour (Tour 1) gives suggestions for congregations wishing to borrow books and have a sampler of the music and text. This is bound to be only a cursory 'toe in the water' exercise, and the points made in the previous sections ('Begin with the words' and 'Think about the music') need to be borne in mind. There is no substitute for a close and detailed look at the material by an individual or a group within the congregation, who can then advise the Church Meeting on its findings.

The Hymnbook Committee, mentioned by name in the Preface to the full Music Edition, are still eager and willing to help congregations if they are uncertain about the ways forward. There should also be individuals from your District and Province who have now become knowledgable about 'Rejoice and Sing' and willing to visit churches. Please don't make your decision on rumour and hearsay!

 eography

There is always a great deal of heart-searching by hymnbook compilers about the shape and format of a new book. If we are to understand 'Rejoice and Sing' we need to look at the table of Contents very closely.

The first twenty 'hymns' form an outline Order of Worship with musical items interspersed. This section can be used in a variety of ways. It is not meant to be a rigid framework. Some of the musical pieces are new and exciting! It reflects the movement in our churches

towards a more 'responsive' form of worship.
Furthermore, it reminds us at the outset this book is
not simply a book of 'hymns'. It is a worship resource.
It will stimulate us and change the way we worship.
(Alleluia!)

Immediately, then, we are
drawn into a spirit of worship.
The place we have come to is
holy! We start with a God
whose 'worth'-ship is our chief
delight and goal.

The focus is not on ourselves
but on GOD. This God has been
made known to us as Creator,
Redeemer and Life-Giver, one God in Trinity. After an
opening section of eighteen hymns (21-38) focussing
specifically on the Trinity, the active outgoing work of
God is explored in detail. Hymns 39-125 sing of God's
creative energy; hymns 126-293 tell of God coming in
Christ; hymns 294-330 proclaim the life-giving power
of God the Holy Spirit. Each of these three sections ends
in a spirit of praise. There are numerous sub-themes
and within these the hymns are all arranged in
alphabetical order.

The picture we should now have of deeply etched on
our minds and hearts is of a God who never tires, a God
who pours out life and joy and hope into the world, a
God who always speaks before we do, weeps before we
do, suffers before we do, and who is ever-living and
ever-victorious. How can we fail to be uplifted!

But now the spotlight falls on us. From hymn 331 we
are drawn to look inwards at our deep need for God and
the challenge to hear and respond to what God is doing
in the world. Here is material which is sensitive,
personal and searching (hymns 331-375).

Our collective response to God's love comes through the
experience we share in the Church. It is to this theme
the book now turns. Hymns 376-598 explore the broad
experience of worship, discipleship and pilgrimage we
share in the Church. Again, sub-sections are in
alphabetical order.

But we are not allowed to stay in 'churchianity'. The Gospel is meant for the world. Hymns 599-655 deal with this outward serving tide by which the love and peace, the justice and healing of God flow into a dangerous and frenetic world. Whereas hymnbooks in the past have given us scant choice, here are riches indeed. The mood is not 'Onward! Christian soldiers' but 'We have no mission but to serve...' (No. 636) and 'Put peace into each other's hands' (No. 635).

A concluding section completes the hymns. Its theme is 'All one in God's eternal praise' (Hymns 656-668). The circle is complete. Praise begins and ends in GOD.

The Psalms and Canticles form a separate section (Nos. 669-758). This is not an appendix! It is separate to give it its true worth. Think of it as Part 2 of the hymnbook! Our Reformed forefathers and foremothers should rejoice and sing at the inclusion of such a rich Psalm section. The Psalms can be sung, recited, and prayed and in countless ways. (See Tour 7 for more ideas on how to use this invaluable section). The Psalms are in numerical order and include prose, metrical and paraphrase, ancient and modern! So also with the Canticles or other scripture passages suitable for reciting and chanting. There is great variety!

Finally; the hymnbook comes to its conclusion with the Apostles' Creed, the Nicene Creed and the responsive statement on the Nature, Faith and Order of the United Reformed Church. The National Anthem makes up the final numbered item at 762.

We cannot leave this brisk gallop through the 'geography' without mention of the Indexes. These are most valuable to those responsible for the preparation of worship. They include an Index of Copyright owners (including on page 1120 a useful list of publishers) for those who wish to write away to clear copyright for reproduction. Then there comes a Thematic index, and one of Biblical Passages. Next comes the Indexes of Authors and Composers, followed by those on Tunes (Alphabetical and Metrical). Finally there is the Index of First Lines (also in the Melody edition).

A few ancient prayers appear on the inside of the front cover and the Lord's Prayer (two version) and Gloria Patri on the inside of the back cover.

Such is the shape and form of 'Rejoice and Sing'. It always takes people some tine to get to grips with a new book like this. But it is worth it! The tours which follow later will look at various sections of the hymnbook, making practical suggestions. They will also cross sections and cover some of the themes which are not so easy to track down.

ᗰeather

What's the weather going to be like? Shall I take an umbrella? This must be the most common question asked before setting out on any trip to a strange place.

Well what's the climate like when you make your home with 'Rejoice and Sing'? The answer must be: 'be prepared for anything!'

The main atmosphere of the book is one of joy. But it is not a superficial joy. The joy is not a 'I am H.A.P.P.Y' sort of joy. It does not ignore the suffering and wounds of the world or the difficult questions which torture the human spirit. The joy comes through the deep faith that God is active, compassionate and will never abandon the world. We can enter into this spirit of hopeful joy by embracing the message of these hymns.

Be prepared, however, for faith to be stretched and ideas to grow. There is much of comfort but there is equally the cutting edge of the Gospel. As our language changes so our perceptions need to be examined. Hymns do shape the language of faith. 'Rejoice and Sing' may make us think again about what we believe as well as how we act. In fact, the communal and the personal are held in careful balance. We are not allowed to wallow in our own need for salvation for God is 'out there' in the world calling us to commitment and service. And yet there is no shortage of hymns invoking deep emotion and intensity (see Tour 11). Be prepared to meet a God who steps out ahead of us, no matter what mood we are in or what our expectations may appear to be.

Oh, I forgot the thunderstorms! There are bound to be times when we feel angry because 'our' favourite tune or hymn is not there. Remember, when you are running for cover another person may be sunning themselves on the beach! Then, there's the altering of familiar words. You may want to call down a lightning strike on those who allowed the word 'things' to replace 'sons' in the penultimate line of 'Hark! the herald angels sing' (No.159), but generally there has been a great deal of what the Committee called 'invisible mending' to make our language more inclusive. Future hymn book compilers may have much to rejoice and sing over when they see how much useful work has been done. They can have a fresh 'go' at the places where *Rejoice and Sing* has fallen short.

etting about

Travel in a foreign country can be hazardous. You need to be very careful. Hiring a car gives you greater freedom but you must remember that you may be driving on the other side of the road.

A new hymn book is uncharted territory. Attention must be given to the framework of the book (See above section: Geography). Get a feel for the shape of the book and keep an eye on the headings on the top of the page. In the full music edition the headings on the top of the left hand pages are the main section headings. The right hand pages give the headings of the sub-sections.

The Indexes are the most valuable means of transporting us around. Some of these can now be dealt with in more detail:

1. Index of Themes

This is found from page 1121 of the Full Music Edition. The themes are gathered in alphabetical order. They include themes which are already sub-sections in the main framework. This is in order that additional suggestions of hymns for those sections can be provided.

Those involved in the preparation of worship will be helped by this index but will also have some frustrating moments! The theme you want may be there under a different heading! Or it may not be there at all!

Here are ten tips:

i)   Lent comes under 'Temptation' and 'Transfiguration' and 'Discipleship'.

ii) Easter comes under 'Resurrection' and 'Praising the Crucified and Risen Lord'.

iii) Pentecost comes under 'The Coming of the Holy Spirit', 'Gifts of the Spirit' and 'Praising the Holy Spirit'.

iv) Harvest is best supplemented by 'Ecology', 'Stewardship', 'Ruler and Guide of Creation' and 'God's Providence'

v)   Love, Joy and Peace are present but there is no Hope! Try themes such as 'Waiting on God', 'Help in Trouble' and 'Trust in God'.

vi) For Communion read 'Lord's Supper'.

vii) For Weddings read 'Marriage' and 'Love'

viii) For Funerals try 'Death', 'Help in Trouble' and 'Courage'.

ix) Christian Education comes under 'Growing in Faith', 'Christ's Example', and 'Wisdom'.

x)   Church and Community themes can be supplemented from 'Freedom', 'Prisoners of Conscience', 'Citizenship', 'Care for all' and 'Service'.

One very useful section of themes is that entitled 'Prayer Responses'. These are the one-verse items which can be used at many points in worship. See Tour 10 for more detail on these.

In the light of all this, you may wish to make your own Index! It must be admitted that some other hymnbooks have better indexes. Don't be afraid to try them alongside this one!

2.   ***Index of Biblical Passages***
This is found on page 1129 of the Full Music Edition. It may not be surprising to discover the extent to which hymn-writers are inspired by Scripture!

There are some of the great hymns of the past in which phrase after phrase bears some allusion to some text from the Bible. '*Hymns and Psalms*', the

Methodist hymn book has forty two pages to its Index of Biblical Texts. *'Rejoice and Sing'* does not attempt to deal as comprehensively as that. The references are to hymns which 'make a significant use of texts'. Not surprisingly the longest section is that of the Psalms.

Again, worship leaders may wish to compile their own extended Scripture index as they make use of the book.

3.

Indexes of Tunes

There are two indexes to help us with tunes.
The first is an Alphabetical Index (pages 1144-1147) and this is followed by a Metrical Index of Tunes (pages 1148-1153).

The Alphabetical list may not be used very often, except by Organists. People don't remember Tune names like they know football teams. (Though some do!) Particularly useful for organists and keyboard players is the way that this Index also informs us when a tune is printed in more than one key. (eg. *Bunessan* ['Morning is broken'] is in D flat at No. 45 and in C in No. 48.

The Metrical Index is the favourite hunting ground for those who want to find an alternative tune. Next to the name of a tune there is usually a note of the metre. This may be a series of numbers or a list of abbreviations. They signify the number of syllables in the lines of the verse. C.M. (Common Metre) is 86.86.; S.M. (Short Metre) is 66.86; L.M. (Long Metre) is 88.88. In addition to these three meters which have specific names there are many other combinations of lines. Very common are the 'eight liners' which are 'double' the normal length. (eg. D.C.M. Double Common Metre).

In choosing an alternative tune it is important to realise that a tune with identical numbers does not guarantee a perfect fit. The stress may be on the wrong syllables. Always try it over ahead of time! Remember also that the words remain the most important ingredient. Find a tune in the right mood and tempo to suit the words.

Index of First Lines and Titles
This is the speediest and most used means of
getting around the hymnbook. It is found on
pages 1154-1171.

This index contains not only the first lines of all the
hymns and psalms but also the titles of the worship
material and the canticles. Where these differ from
the first lines, the titles are put in italics.

The Index compilers have been falling over backwards
to help us. Where the first line of a familiar hymn
has been changed they have kept the original words
in. The hymns which fall into this category have been
put into square brackets. There is an example right at
the beginning. The first hymn under 'A' is 'A fortress
sure is God our King'. It is given the number 585.
Three lines further down is the hymn 'A safe strong-
hold our God is still' This is also given the number
585. You will notice that these two hymns are put in
square brackets. This indicates that the words of the
first line have been altered. If you look up number
585, you will find that the actual first line is 'Our God
stands like a fortress rock'. The compilers have chosen
a translation by Stephen Orchard of the Martin Luther
original. In the Index, 'Our God stands like a fortress
rock' is not in brackets. Since this change has arisen
because a fresh translation has been written there is
'cross' symbol also inserted in the brackets.

Still confused? Try looking up, 'Christ is made the
sure foundation', for another example.

The Index of first lines and titles also contains the
tunes for each hymn and where there is no name for
the tune the composer's name is given.

anguage hints

Some people have a flare for languages and
can turn it on when they are on holiday,
sometimes to the embarrassment of their
closest and dearest! Then there are the tourists who
seem to sport the inbred assumption that 'foreigners'
are uncivilised unless they speak English!

We also need to remember that language is not set in concrete. It is fluid and ever-changing. You cannot go to Greece with six years New Testament Greek and expect to be able to communicate!

So with the language of hymns. The way people spoke in the time of Elizabeth the first is not the same as the way people speak in the age of Elizabeth the second. Moreover language has changed profoundly during the last fifty years. That is because culture has changed. Our attitudes to children, to world neighbours, to space, to the environment, to people of a different faith tradition, all dramatically affect the way we express ourselves.

Here is a hymn from a hymnbook entitled 'Children Praising', first published in 1937 but which had reprints up to 1966. The music editor is Herbert Wiseman and the words are edited by W.H. Hamilton. It is entitled: 'Chinese Children'.

> Chinese children use no spoons
> Clever chopsticks they employ
> Quaint and unfamiliar tunes
> Tell their early voices joy.
> Sisters and brothers therefore we
> To these Chinese children be.
>
> Yet the same great God who gives
> food and songs that make us glad
> with these Chinese children lives,
> loves each lass and loves each lad.
> Sisters and brothers therefore we
> to these Chinese children be.

In some ways this hymn was reaching towards ideas beyond its age. The idea that God is with people of other races and cultures before Christians take them the Gospel is certainly not out of date! The language, however, is 'twee', and a mite patronising! We couldn't imagine singing such a hymn today without suppressing some sniggers.

Missionary hymns from the mid nineteenth century presumed that much of the world lay in thick darkness and that the reason for this was the heathen cultures represented there. Today's world is no less dark! But it is as dark in the United Kingdom as it is in Central Africa! Not surprisingly, therefore, the compilers of 'Rejoice and Sing' have had to adjust the words of certain well loved hymns.

Here is one example: 'Thy kingdom come, O God'
(R & S. 638; Congregational Praise 584; Church
Hymnary III 322). The last verse used to read:

> O'er heathen lands afar
>   Thick darkness broodeth yet;
> Arise, O Morning Star,
>   Arise, and never set.

In 'Rejoice and Sing', this now becomes:

> O'er lands both near and far
>   thick darkness broodeth yet;
> arise, O Morning Star,
>   arise, and never set!

Here is a good example of 'invisible mending', by which
the thought-pattern becomes contemporary with a
minimum of alteration to the words.

The compilers have not tried to take out all archaic
language. The words 'thee' and 'thy' and 'thine' are
usually retained because it would disturb the poetic flow
too much to change the hymn. Sometimes, however,
'you' and 'your' can be inserted without anyone realising
(eg. No. 321: 'Your words to me are life and health').

In some instances there has been an attempt to improve
the sense of a hymn. Even some of our most popular
hymns can be confusing! Look, for instance at the
excellent Ascension Day hymn 'At the Name of Jesus'
(No. 261). Have the compilers improved the sense for
you? (I can hear you saying: 'I never had a problem!')

Travellers into 'Rejoice and Sing' country can expect
all types and shades of language, from the most
contemporary to the most ancient. There will be a
few surprises when the 'words committee' have tried
to be faithful to the General Assembly's resolution that
inclusive language should be the norm in United
Reformed Church publications. In some places there
have been some tasteful amendments. Verse 3 of
'It came upon the midnight clear' (No. 145) now reads:

> 'and we, at bitter war, hear not
> the love-song which they bring:
> O hush the noise and end the strife
> to hear the angels sing.'

In other places, the wording has not come out so sweetly. Brian Wren's rewrite of 'There's a spirit in the air' (No. 329) replaces the couplet:

> 'God in Christ has come to stay.
> We can see his power today'.

with

> 'God in Christ has come to stay.
> Live tomorrow's life today.'

Let's not dwell any longer on these bits and pieces. As you travel you will have many occasions for smiling but there may be times to grimace as well. Remember that we can't turn the clock back. We must continue to strive to communicate in the best contemporary language rather than the words of past generations.

Praise God we have some excellent hymn-writers who can put the Gospel into a language which is challenging and sensitive. If the people of tomorrow are to sing God's praise they may well hear discover that music not in the preaching of the twentieth century but in the poetry of its hymn-writers.

 ountry Code

When you go on vacation you may leave your brains at home on the television but you must not leave your manners! Respecting the countryside is one such elementary obligation. The Country Code says 'don't drop litter' and 'don't pick wild-flowers' and 'shut gates after you'. These apply no matter whether you are holidaying in Scotland or in Crete.

Can we construct a Code for approaching a new hymn-book? Let's try:

First, for congregations:

1. Remember that the aim is to 'Worship' effectively. The Hymnbook is a resource to help us 'offer the best'.

2. When you look up the numbers before the service starts, don't ask 'Do I know the tune?' but 'What is this hymn saying to me?'

3. Don't be afraid of singing! If you sing a wrong note God will not strike you with a bolt of lightning.
4. Try and sing at the same speed as the organist or pianist played when s/he played the hymn through beforehand.
5. Think about the words as you sing.
6. If you don't know the tune and there has been no attempt before worship to teach the hymn, then make a note of the number and ask the organist if it can be taught at some point.
7. Help young children follow the words and tune.
8. Keep an eye open for elderly members who cannot find the place.
9. Take a book home and read it.
10. Smile, God loves you.

Second, for leaders of worship:

1. Make sure you have your own copy of the Full Music Edition.
2. Read it, (a bit at a time with a glass of wine).
3. Plan ahead.
4. Meet with your music leaders regularly. Agree on what hymns need to be taught and which can be used at any time.
5. Use the book as a full worship resource.
6. Vary your choice of hymns. Vary the meters.
7. Look carefully at each hymn you have chosen and ask how best the hymn can be communicated. Can a singing group sing certain verses? Or a soloist? Should the congregation sit or stand?
8. Be clear in your directions in worship. Allow time for people to find their places.
9. If you are singing loud into the microphone, don't sing the harmony! Sing the melody. Better still, don't sing into the microphone. You are not Tom Jones or Shirley Bassey!
10. Be encouraging. Smile: the hymn book committee loves you!

Third, for organists, choirleaders, and reluctant musicians:

1. Play through the whole book. (Then there is a chance that the book will stay open on the music stand!) If it doesn't, consider suicide. Then devise a Heath-Robinson contraption to keep the book in place. (Most people use rubber bands, some use enormous close pegs!)

2. Meet with the worship leader(s) regularly.
3. When you receive the hymns, read through the words as well as the tune.
4. Work out where the climax of each hymn comes. Which parts are loud and soft? Discuss with the worship leader how the hymn can be communicated musically.
5. Decide at what speed you wish the hymn to be sung. Play the 'play through' at that speed. Then keep to that speed for each verse, willy nilly! Rhythm and vitality are more important than volume.
6. In the 'play through' consider playing the first line of the hymn in unison so that it gives a clear indicator of the tune to the congregation.
7. If there are prayer responses, decide how these are going to be introduced.
8. If the hymn is well known, you do not need to play the melody fortissimo. You can even leave it out, and accompany the congregation with the lower parts.
9. If you are an organist then encourage other instrumental playing, so that there is more participation of all age groups in the musical leadership.
10. Be positive. Smile: the minister loves you!

istorical Monuments

You may not go on holiday in order to be steeped in history, but in most locations you will not be able to avoid the treasured past of the people and culture which you are visiting.

The same will apply in any relationship you may have with a new hymn book. Hymn books do not start from 'cold'. The arise out of a particular context. If you visit England you cannot get away from cathedrals! Similarly, if you visit a new Reformed Church Hymn Book you will not be able to get away from the Reformation or from Isaac Watts or from the more recent history of the United Reformed Church, its life and its attempt to be the church.

'*Rejoice and Sing*' did have the freedom to say 'no' to the
past. It was not a revision of a previous hymn book.
It did start from scratch. But it couldn't avoid the story
of the three denominations from which it had grown.

The Presbyterian tradition, for instance, stressed the
importance of 'the Word of God' which was proclaimed
in worship and which was responded to by the
congregation. Not surprisingly, the decision of the
Hymn book committee to place the Psalm section on its
own and therefore to give it prominence (as I said before,
as a 'Part 2' of the Hymn book) reflects this strand from
the past. It may also be reflected in the preference the
committee had for Biblical 'choruses' rather than those
which had words which were trite: "Lord, I really want
to love you..." and therefore would have a very short
shelf-life.

The Congregational tradition, could stress individual
commitment and piety, as well as the freedom to be
creative and imaginative in worship. These traditions
have emerged in the new hymnbook also. There are
many hymns voicing individual response to God and
the willingness of the book to break new ground in
language and in the works of contemporary writers
and composers is ample evidence of the free spirit so
noticeable in the past. The stress of all our Free Church
traditions to be active in society and to take seriously
justice and peace issues has led to a very strong section
on these issues within the book.

Finally, the Churches of Christ brought to the United
Reformed Church three 'treasures': believer's Baptism,
a weekly celebration of the Lord's Supper, and a pattern
of non-stipendiary ministry. '*Rejoice and Sing*' has a rich
and comprehensive section on both sacraments. Baptism
and the Lord's Supper are not minor sections but central
pillars of the new book. The hymns on the church,
moreover, stress the ministry of the whole people of
God and the need to search for new patterns of ministry
for the future church.

We could say much more about these themes. But let
us go back a little further for a moment. Many people
believe that 'hymn writing' actually began with Martin
Luther. Certainly it was reborn through his genius.
'*Rejoice and Sing*', however, will not allow you to imagine
hymns didn't exist before the Reformation. There is a

splendid selection of hymns from the early centuries of Christianity, and the Historical Tour will point you in the direction of some of these.

Hymn singing goes back to the creation! The morning stars had a hymn book! The moon and the sun broadcast 'Songs of praise!' We are simply tuning in to what has been on the airwaves for generations. If the commercial world can rediscover the worth of Gregorian Chants, then the church needs to be doubly aware of the riches which come from the past. It is no good simply clinging to the hymns of the immediately previous generation. What we need is to treasure the best from every century and to offer the best from our own time, so that the 'Hallelujah' rings down the ages and the world is moved to deeds of praise.

Recent Changes

All this now brings us to the present scene. The fact is, we live in the present. When we go and visit Rome, we might wish upon a star that we could see it as it was in the time of Claudius but we know that is not possible. If we travel to a remote island in the Pacific in the hope of viewing it through the eyes of the first visitors by boat a thousand years ago, that would be a foolish aspiration. Rome will be full of honking traffic and the Pacific Island will contain people who watch 'Neighbours' (a few episodes ahead of the UK!)

Any hymnbook needs to deal with the present realities of the world, and although hymns must be chosen with the hope that they will not simply reflect passing fads and gimmicks, there must be a genuine attempt to address the present.

'Rejoice and Sing's' attempts to break new ground in respect of inclusive language is part of this need to deal positively with the present. It has also tried to choose some of the best of contemporary writing and had literally thousands of submissions offering new material, never hitherto published. Inevitably, excellent material missed the boat as far as publication is concerned. That will always be the case, for sooner than later the manuscript has to go to press!

One of the tours (No. 5: 'Hidden Gems') contains quite a lot of new material. The United Reformed Church has been particularly blessed by its own authors, translators and composers who are in the forefront of this global creativity.

 irst Aid

Here are a few common illnesses and problems you may encounter.

Insect Bites: There are bound to be a number of people who bite back when a new Hymnbook is published. They can be painful. The best antidote is a sense of humour. Remember "Guide me O Thou great Jehovah" was new once! If they persist, or begin to swarm with "wherzzzzzzzzzz onward Christian Soldierzzzzzzzzzzzzz" then remind them that there were many hymns in the "old book" which they didn't know.

Indigestion: The new diet can be a bit rich: a bit too spicy for bland UK tastes. The solution may be to go back to the meat and two veg sort of diet with "the Church's one foundation" or "Summer suns are glowing", but a quick reminder that most jolly Christmas carols were once dances might convince the stomach to accept more festive fare.

Montezumer's Revenge: (A Mexican description of problems with the water, leading to a mild form of dysentery!) This might affect the choir or the more operatic of Church members. It is a case of getting the runs. When musical people feel they have to have the elaborations of harmony and descant in order to survive, then remind them that the majority of the members have not been members of the Huddersfield Choral Society, and that if the church is to grow, then, (alas) the chance of the Cambridge Singers suddenly applying for membership of your church is very slim. More likely than not new members in their twenties and thirties will not be able to sing at all. Let the choir sing a verse on their own from time to time!

Sunburn: This is the most common of complaints. It comes from basking in the glow of the sun for too long without adequate preparation. So don't choose five new hymns a week when you have purchased the new hymnbook. Take it gently. Introduce new material gradually. Then it will give people that warm and relaxed feeling.

Jelly Fish: These are far worse than insect bites (see above). Jelly fish inject a poison which can ruin your whole holiday. They can even be fatal. So avoid at all costs. In any church there will be someone who will want to sabotage the whole operation. The best thing is to ignore them. Swim in safer waters. They will have attacked before when the Youth Club broke a window or the children asked if they could share in the communion service.

Lifeguards: Beware of bronzed, good looking salesmen of the new hymnbook. They may look good but you will be better off with someone who knows what it is you will be getting into and knows how to swim.

Cramp: Don't swim in cold water. A church which is cold in its welcome and cold in its relationships will have a hard job coping with a new hymnbook.

Intoxication: You cannot sell a new hymnbook unless you know its weaknesses as well as its strengths. *'Rejoice and Sing'* is good. But it is not perfect! You will not convert the sceptics by over-enthusing, when there are some clear shortcomings. Be positive, but be honest and sober in your appraisal. Ask people to tell you their views.

Jet-Lag: This is an uncomfortable and distressing illness experienced by all who try to cross the time boundaries. A new hymnal is bound to trigger a certain amount of disorientation for those who adopt it cannot imagine they are living in their previous surroundings. If you step into something new, then you have to accept the new time scale. You cannot imagine you are living on the old time. In other words, you cannot travel into the land of a new and exciting hymn book and still keep on referring to the tunes in the 'old' book. Perhaps there will be a time of great discomfort for you are in new surroundings but that is where you now live. Enjoy it! (You will discover your normal sleep pattern again!)

Lost keys: Make sure the piano has all the keys. It sounds better that way.

Lost children: Don't imagine that the new hymn book is only for adults. It is for the whole church family. Children and adults together discover their faith and deepen it through exploring the hymn book. Take time to help each person find their way around. Children will help us use the book imaginatively. Whatever you do, don't limit children to the 'first two hymns' which in some churches will always be a hymn of praise and a so-called 'children'`s hymn' (yuk!). A balanced diet is necessary. Explore the whole book!

Sick bags: These will be found in the pocket in front of you on all flights. Put in it those hymns which make you......(There are some in every hymn book.)

Pickpockets: Beware of those who steal from others. Stealing another person's words and music is a very common occurrence. Sometimes this is allowed by composers and writers but if it is not indicated on the copy then you must seek permission. Copyright laws may seem to be a nuisance but they do protect the hard work of others. In '*Rejoice and Sing*' the owners of the copyright for music and words are listed on pages 1113 - 1120 and sometimes at the foot of the page where the hymn is located.

There are probable many more, but please don't let this talk of pitfalls put you off the journey, because...

...it's time....to tour.

The Tours

ou have read the introduction. Now its time to hit the road. The rest of this little book offers you a number of tours which will help you get the most out of *'Rejoice and Sing'*.

You now have an opportunity to make some choices and to move around the rest of the book in whatever order is most helpful to you.

The tours illustrate the fact that the new hymn book is a magnificent resource. It would be possible to make a tour out of individual hymns, so rich are some in poetry, in beauty, in spiritual insight and in practical challenge. The number of journeys is therefore limitless and you will make your own discoveries. Please use these simply as a beginning. You will want to return to see more and more.

Here they are in summary:

TOUR 1: Introductory

The hymns chosen for this will enable you to get a taste for the general flavour of the book. Many of the hymns will be found in other tours as well. Good for services which are of the 'Songs of Praise' type and which are designed to help people discover hymns new and old which they will come to enjoy.

TOUR 2: Historical

There are hymns in *'Rejoice and Sing'* from almost every century. Music and words cross the generations. People have always been inspired to write and to sing. This tour will focus upon some of these 'hymns through the ages' and show how the compilers of the hymn book have tried to give us a rich choice to enjoy.

TOUR 3: All-age

The hymn book is not a book for adults only! Children and young people need to discover it for themselves and this tour is included to enable them to do this. It is vital to realise that every tour is for adults and children together. We do not give to children a partial diet of what used to be known as 'children's hymns'. All ages need to discover the historical treasures, the psalms, the hymns for communion, the prayer responses, and so on. But 'Rejoice and sing' does have a plethora of material which is particularly suitable when children are present in worship, so these have been highlighted in this tour section.

TOUR 4: Special Occasions

The Christian year forms the framework for our worship occasions but worship leaders and musicians sometimes need help in choosing hymns and psalms for special Sundays such as Harvest, Remembrance, your 178th Anniversary and so on! These tours will help unearth some goodies for such occasions.

TOUR 5: Hidden Gems

No matter how long you have had a hymn book, you will always be discovering new treasures as time passes. Here are some of the hidden 'gems' which need a little deeper digging for. They may not sparkle at first! Some may need some hard work polishing. But it will be worth it.

TOUR 6: Global

'Rejoice and Sing' is not as strong as some recent hymn books on its international hymns. It is very 'western' in its choices. The recent Methodist, Presbyterian and United Church of Christ hymnals in the United States have a greater breadth of global music. All the more reason therefore to make the most of what is on offer in 'Rejoice and Sing'. This tour helps us discover the hymns from many parts of the world which have found their way into our new hymn book.

TOUR 7: Psalms

There is already a danger that the Psalm section is going to be the least used. That would be a disaster, for this is a magnificent resource for reading and for singing. For too long the singing of Psalms has been the task of choirs and therefore, as choirs have died out, so has the singing of the Psalms. This tour will try and put that to rights!

TOUR 8: Words Only

Here is a tour around some of the material in the hymn book which is most suitable for reading in public worship. Many hymns started their life as poems. One of the reasons that *Rejoice and Sing* does not have the words printed between the staves of music (like most hymn books in the United States) is that the words need to be seen to have an existence of their own. We have an opportunity to make the most of the words in worship. This tour shows how.

TOUR 9: A Capella

What a fancy name! No its not a tour around the Latin hymns! One of the best way to sing hymns is to sing them without the accompaniment of another instrument. In fact, if you are learning any new hymn it is the very best way of learning! Some hymns are particularly suitable for 'a capella' singing. This includes the 'rounds' which could have appeared in the 'Words Only' tour (No. 8) but which are located here instead.

TOUR 10: Short Excursions

There has been a rebirth of one verse 'responses' in recent hymn books. The compilers of *Rejoice and Sing* felt that our worship has been enriched greatly in the last decade by the prayer responses which have come from Taizé and from Iona, as well as those written by our own composers. This tour looks at suitable material for singing in this way, including short liturgical items and antiphons. Omitted are the 'rounds' which are in the 'A Capella' tour (No. 9)

The final tour focusses on the material in the hymn book which is helpful for private devotion. Many hymns and psalms are very personal. They are for reading quietly at home or before the start of Sunday worship. Some worship occasions which involve healing or silence, or take place in a more intimate atmosphere may use the hymns and psalms highlighted in this tour. The tourbook ends on a directly personal note. *'Rejoice and Sing'* is the community's book but the individual's also. It is both global and intensely personal at the same time.

Tour 1 : Introductory

Introduction:

n introductory tour needs careful thought. Ask of your particular congregation: "What are their expectations?" The following suggestions cannot possibly meet all circumstances. You will need to adjust selection of hymns and psalms to meet your own needs.

Don't put too much in to a particular occasion. Remember the danger of sunburn! (First Aid hints earlier!) It is a better idea to plan a series of occasions rather than try and concentrate on a single one.

This tour will have to be self-organised from a general list of hymns and psalms which are particularly suitable. The reason for selection is put alongside each hymn. It is quite a long list! Make your own suggestions from it, remembering to select a variety pack, with differing lengths of verse, differing metre and so on.

General List:

14b: **'Lamb of God'**
Found in the initial order of service, this new 'round' is easily picked up. Learn the main tune one week in unison. Repeat on the next week and then try it in two-part canon. Sing it quietly! Always remember the meaning of the words.

30:   **'Father, we love you, we worship and adore you'**
This popular meditative chorus also has guitar chords; try different voices for the verse, quartet or solos; again, make it quiet.

64: **'I lift my eyes to the quiet hills'**
*This hymn has an excellent melody line, and is good
solo material; make sure the singing is smooth and
the phrases carry through to preserve the meaning.
Can be played through on piano with the words of the
hymn spoken at the same time. A good way to introduce
the hymn.*

95: **'God is love: let heaven adore him'**
*Fine words by Timothy Rees to a popular Welsh tune;
Verse 1 can be (f) loud; verse two needs to diminuendo
so that it ends very quietly. Verse three then starts very
quiet and ends back at loud (f). A good example of
texture in singing.*

107: **'The love of God comes close'**
*Another good Welsh tune; Iona words fit well; try and
get some variety. Read the hymn aloud first, giving the
last three lines of each verse to the whole congregation
with the rest given to solo voices. It can be sung in this
way too.*

108: **'The love of God is broad like beach
and meadow'**
*Refreshing and singable melody and words from Sweden;
goes well with guitar accompaniment. Verse three should
be quieter than the others. The chorus can be used as a
prayer response on its own.*

178: **'Who would think that what was needed'**
*'Scarlet ribbons' fits remarkably well to these strong
Christmas words. Variety can be achieved by the
congregation humming the middle verse and a solo voice
singing the words. Instrumental descant with flute or
oboe will be particularly effective.*

186: **'Lord, when the wise men came from far'**
*An excellent tune not in our previous books; fascinating
Epiphany words, which need some unpacking!
They need reading first and pondering! The tune is
simple in comparison!*

188: **'Born in the night'**
*What a beautiful melody! it can be accompanied by
guitar and other instruments. Again the unison may
be supplemented by a hummed or "oo-ed" harmony,
but it must not take away from the exquisite melody.
Verse three ends quietly but is transformed by the start
of verse 4.*

200: **'The kingdom of God is justice and joy'**
Here are two good tunes very different from each other.
'Out Skerries' is a challenge and needs a good
accompanist! It is already proving popular. Piano is
better than organ. (Paul Bateman suggests that both
organ and piano together is ideal!) Tetherdown is no
less joyful a hymn and must not drag. Whichever tune
is sung the spirit of joy must make the words dance.

243: **'Now the green blade rises from the
buried grain'**
A haunting Easter hymn with meaningful Easter words.
Introduce the hymn with a solo recorder, oboe or flute.
The hymn does not need 'full organ'. It can sound
beautiful unaccompanied.

318: **'Not far beyond the sea, nor high'**
If you knew this from 'New Church Praise', you will
notice that George Caird's brilliant hymn now has a
second verse of his added. It can be read as a prayer.
The singing is demanding on the lungs if we are to
make sense of the fine words.

319: **'Thanks to God whose word was spoken'**
RT Brooks has written some splendid words to the
familiar tune: 'Regent Square'. The hymn is a sermon
and could be fitted with readings verse by verse!
It fits the heading 'The Word and the Spirit' admirably.

401: **'Through our lives and by our prayers,
your kingdom come'**
This is a prayer response from Iona. A three note
ascending arpeggio in D major can help its introduction
between prayers.

402: **'Ubi caritas et amor'**
Here is a worship response from Taizé, easily learnt
and unforgettable. Try and help people get their mouths
round the Latin words! (Ubi is pronounced 'oobi' and
Deus is 'Day-oos'. If the response is repeated a number
of times then it should be varied in its dynamics, perhaps
sung at a whisper after a prayer covering human pain
etc. It is very effective unaccompanied.

422: **'Lift high the Cross, the love of Christ proclaim'**
A processional hymn for confirmation and many other occasions. It can also be made into a whole order of service! The response can be used separately from the hymn, as a prayer response in other contexts. The danger of the hymn is that it is often sung 'multo belto' (pardon the Italian), when some of the verses have a painful and sharp message. Try and achieve contrast by making verses 2 and 3 quiet. If you can add a trumpet this hymn can send shivers down your spine!

438: **'An upper room did our Lord prepare'**
'Rejoice and Sing' makes use of a number of folk melodies. The music edition includes some suggestions on how to sing this with soloists or 'semichorus'. Think of how this fine hymn can be used at communion.

474: **'Brother, sister, let me serve you'**
A hymn written from the present generation! The author is from New Zealand. The guitar chords may have had to be printed for copyright reasons but are impracticable and can be ignored! If you look carefully at the beautiful words then you can see that verses 2 and 5 are in the plural and the other verses in the first person singular. The hymn lends itself to solo singing especially on verses 3 & 4. If you have male and female soloists singing these verses from different parts of the sanctuary then this can be most effective. The hymn needs gentle treatment and is to be sung and played quietly. Organists who do not adore four sharps may prefer to play this in three flats!

504: **'Light of the world, from whom all truth proceeding'** or
660: **'Hark what a sound and too divine for hearing'**
R R Terry's tune, 'Highwood', made popular on BBC 'Songs of Praise' is chosen for both these sets of words. The words of 660 are probably the easiest set with which to learn the tune, for the phrasing is shorter.

522: **'From heaven you came, helpless babe'**
Perhaps the best known of Graham Kendrick's hymns, this will probably be known already. It is very popular for ordinations and inductions! Verse 2 can be sung pianissimo by an individual or small singing group. Verse 3 also needs to be very quiet. The chorus too could be sung quietly after these verses, rather than coming in with full organ (or orchestra)!

530: **'Living God, your joyful Spirit'**
Jill Jenkins of Palmers Green wrote these words, excellent
for anniversaries and many other occasions. The hymn
will be helped by some variety in dynamics, with verses
2 & 3 more reflective. The hymn also reads well as a
prayer. You may well need to practise the last line.
The third note from the end is lower than you think.
Make sure you go down to the 'd'.

548: **'Nothing distress you'**
Colin Thompson's brilliant translation of Teresa of
Avila's poem is one of the gems you may meet on another
tour! Note how the words of each line in verse one
appear in the following verses, matching the original
author's intentions. Those familiar with Taizé material
will also know 'Nada te turbe' as a beautiful prayer
response available in their publications. Peter Cutts' tune
lends itself to solo oboe or flute, bringing out the lyrical
melody. When learning this hymn try playing the tune
and having a 'solo' reader speak the words over the
music, following the phrasing. The full beauty of the
words will come across and the music will become
familiar in the background.

558: **'Will you come and follow me'**
This is another example of a folk melody becoming a
pleasing hymn. John Bell and Graham Maule of the
Iona Community have enriched our hymnody immensely
through recovering airs like this. The hymn should not
be sung too fast, but it should maintain its 'jagged'
rhythm.

603: **'Lord, for the years your love has kept
and guided'**
The metre of this hymn is 11.10.11.10., the same as 504
and 660, so don't choose both in the same service. The
tune was written for these words and has a good joyful
rhythm. Make sure the syncopation is kept at the end
of line one. Verse 4 provides a contrast in mood which
should be matched by quiet singing. It can be sung
unaccompanied. Since the tune starts on a unison C this
is particularly suitable for 'a capella' singing.

633: **'O let us spread the pollen of peace
throughout the land'**
A folk-song-hymn, best sung to guitar with other
instruments added. The rhythm is not as easy as it
appears at first sight. The verse would best suit a duet.
In the chorus, the words 'let us', which repeat three
times, are in quick time, followed by a fourth 'let us'
(after 'cease') in strict time.)

635: **'Put peace into each other's hands'**
This is a deeply moving hymn by Fred Kaan to a
beautiful old tune. It needs to be sung in a reflective,
gentle way. The compilers must have been tempted to
put this in the 'Lord's Supper' section but were wise to
keep it in a wider context of justice and peace. It can
be sung in many contexts.

650: **'God with humanity made one'**
David Fox has penned very special words which can
be read as well as sung. 'Gonfalon Royal' is one of
the best long metre tunes but it is surprising how many
people are still learning it for the first time. It is one
of the few tunes where the 'Amen' is obligatory, so the
congregation needs to be prepared for it.

725: **'I lift my eyes to the hills'**
Not to be confused with No.64! This is a good 'starter'
for learning to sing a 'tone' psalm, with a very singable
Antiphon from Brenda Stephenson. On page 958 of the
full music edition there are some explanations about
Psalm singing including a few lines on how to sing
tone' psalms. The best starting off point is to teach
the Antiphon to the congregation. Then use a group of
singers or soloist to get the hang of the verses. The final
stage is to have the congregation sing the verses.
Remember the words can still be read responsively with
the antiphon, if so desired.

731: **'You are before me, Lord, you are behind'**
Psalm 139, in metrical form by Ian Pitt-Watson.
The words are beautifully phrased and can be used in
worship on their own. The tune 'Sursum Corda' should
be reasonably well known. Don't let it drag! Keep strict
time at the ends of each line. Verses two and three form
a unity and therefore would benefit from a minimum
break between the verses

758: **'Great and Wonderful'**
Here are words from the book of Revelation for reading
responsively in worship. It is included in this list as a
reminder of the resources found in 'Rejoice and Sing'
for reading in worship.

Tour 2: Historical

 here is certainly no need to be bored by the history of hymns. The people of faith have always expressed themselves in song and no mainstream hymnbook can ignore the riches of hymnwriting which every century holds. Although Protestants look to Martin Luther as the founder of hymn-singing in their churches, their eyes are now searching further into history and the discoveries are exciting. *'Rejoice and Sing'* contains many more ancient hymns than the hymnbooks of recent years and this tour will unearth hymns from the saints in every age.

Let it be said that we have to be prepared to adjust our musical tastes, especially as we encounter the most ancient of texts. They are not always set to what we consider popular melodies, though with the rebirth of popularity of hymns in the minor key, we should be better prepared to receive some of the mediaeval versions. The compilers of *'Rejoice and Sing'* have often chosen tunes from the era in which the hymn was written.

If you are to embark on this tour then be prepared to meet some characters from history who have contributed a great deal to our faith. The hymns of the past are the singing of the saints. It may lead you to search for more information about what made these personalities tick. The fact that their names are at the bottom of a hymn page is only the beginning of the story.

As in the case of the previous tour, you may choose from the following comprehensive list. It covers in chronological order much of the material in *'Rejoice and Sing'* up to the year 1700. Space has meant the omission of a few major names: Thomas Aquinas, Paul Gerhardt and John Bunyan, for example. After 1700 you are on your own! With Watts, Doddridge, Wesley to follow you have a plethora of material. Use the Index to locate their hymns.

1st Century

750: **'All praise to thee, for thou, O King divine'**
Although this hymn is from this century, it is based upon
Philippians 2.5-11. This passage from Paul gives us a
glimpse at what may have been one of the earliest of
Christian hymns. Look it up in a modern translation
and you will see that the form of it is basically a two
verse hymn. Any historical exploration needs to remind
people that hymns were sung in Jesus' day (the Psalms)
and that the first friends of Jesus soon started to sing
in worship. This particular hymn can be sung to the set
tune, with its excellent 'Alleluia' refrain, or if you wish
to start off with the more familiar, try 'Sine Nomine' at
No. 658

1st or 2nd Centuries

444: **'Father, we give you thanks, who planted'**
This hymn is based upon a text from the Didache, a
book of Christian teaching from the end of the first
century. Placed in the 'Lord's Supper' section it speaks
of the way Jesus feeds his people and watches over the
world wide Church. It is also a suitable hymn for the
Week of Prayer for Christian Unity. The tune offered
('Les Commandements de Dieu') is worth learning but
an alternative tune is offered from the same sixteenth
century French collection (Rendez à Dieu, No. 709) which
then makes the hymn into two verses of eight lines.

2nd Century

527: **'Jesus, our mighty Lord'**
Based on a text from Clement of Alexandria, these are
magnificent words. Sung to the Welsh tune 'Moab' they
have great dignity. Sung to the alternative tune 'Monks
Gate' (No. 557) they will have a different feel! Verse two
makes a good Benediction/Dismissal.

3rd or 4th Centuries

27: **'Hail, gladdening light of his pure glory poured'**
One of the best known ancient hymns, though not sung
as much today (probably owing to the demise of evening
worship!) It still makes a fine beginning to public
worship. It needs to be sung "in free rhythm"; in other
words, as you would naturally speak the words. So
speak it out loud first. Stress the words you would
normally stress in speaking. Sing it like that.

454: **'Let all mortal flesh keep silence'**
Another communion hymn but this time set to a carol melody 'Picardy' which can dance along. Fits in well with a sermon on Isaiah 6.

462: **'From glory to glory advancing'**
Whereas the previous hymn is suitable for the outset of the communion service, this one, from the same Liturgy of St James, fits well at the end. The tune, finishing as it does on a top E natural, ('service on high!') may put some people off. Look, alas, in the metrical index of tunes and this is the last one: the only one in this metre! Don't give up. Please give it a go.

101: **'O matchless beauty of our God'**
529: **'Light of the minds that know him'**
539: **'How blest are all the saints, our God'**
Three hymns by contemporary authors based on texts by Augustine. Three contemporary authors and translators have done us a great service in leading us into the heart and mind of one of the greatest saints.

No. 101 by Colin Thompson is a masterpiece, speaking eloquently of the beauty of God's presence.

No. 529 by Timothy Dudley-Smith, is quite a contrast in mood but no less attractive. Verse 3 could be sung as a solo. No. 539 penned by Alan Gaunt picks up the wonderful Augustinian thought in which he pictures the soul's journey as a vessel at sea not resting until it finds its rest in God.

537: **'O splendour of God's glory bright'**
Ambrose of Milan was one of the leading hymn writers of the early church. Only one of the twelve hymns usually ascribed to him appears in 'Rejoice and Sing' and it is a 'must' on our historic tour. Ambrose wrote for the Canonical Hours and this is clearly a morning hymn to be sung at sunrise!

5th Century

363: **'Lord Jesus, think on me'**

Synesius, Bishop of the barbarian province of Cyrene, was a philosopher and intellectual, trained in philosophy in Alexandria. Yet nothing could be simpler than this hymn, filled as it is with humility and humanity. The tune, from the sixteenth century, compliments it perfectly in simplicity.

172: **'From east to west, from shore to shore'**

Sedulius is almost unknown. This hymn is part of an acrostic poem and is translated by John Ellerton, better known as the author of 'The day Thou gavest, Lord, is ended'. Its tune is identical to 171, and the words are not very different either.

5th and 6th Centuries

36: **'I bind unto myself today'**
79: **'This day God gives me'**

St Patrick's Breastplate is a well known piece of armour. There are two hymns in 'Rejoice and Sing' based upon the words of this popular Irish saint. The longer version is a marathon and needs more than four or five in the congregation. It is truly majestic when planned well and led strongly. Verse 5, whose tune is 'Clonmacnoise', may be sung by a small choir or quartet, to provide contrast. No. 79 provides a very different setting. James Quinn's words go well to 'Addington'.

6th Century

73: **'O God, thou art the Father'**
272: **'Christ is the world's Redeemer'**

One hymn in two parts marks the contribution of St Columba to 'Rejoice and Sing' Together the words offer praise to the Trinity, finishing in the marvellous last verse of 272: 'Amen - so let it be!' Nevertheless, each hymn can stand on its own. The Irish melody to 272 ('Moville') is attractive and worth learning.

216: **'As royal banners are unfurled'**
228: **'Here proclaim the glorious battle'**
322: **'Welcome, Day of the Lord'**

Venantius Fortunatus was an Italian exile with poetic gifts who became Bishop of Poitiers. He wrote many hymns though the main volume has been lost.
Three are included in 'Rejoice and Sing', two of them newly 'translated' by Alan Gaunt.

No. 216 contains battle-language which is graphic.
You can almost feel the Roman legions marching.
It is set to the French seventeenth century tune
'Solemnis haec festivitas'.

No. 228 has a similar theme, and Alan Gaunt's gift with
words provides us with another splendid hymn. Most
congregations will find 'Picardy' at No. 457 a preferred
alternative to the set tune, though the plain song 'Pange
Lingua' grows on you.

No. 322 is quite different and, thanks to Vaughan
Williams' magnificent tune, gives us a joyful hymn of
celebration for Pentecost. Verses 3 & 5 can be sung by
the choir or a small group, who may be able to dance
through the triplets more gracefully than a large
congregation. Portions of this hymn are eminently
suitable for a Pentecost Introit.

6th and 7th Centuries

254: **'Sing we triumphant hymns of praise'**
It is good to have a hymn in 'Rejoice and Sing' from the
Venerable Bede. It can be sung any Sunday, though it is
particularly appropriate for the period of Easter and
Ascension. The tune 'Church Triumphant' needs to be
played triumphally and brightly as its name suggests.
In verse 2, lines two and three must be sung in one breath
(up to 'where'), and similarly in verse 3, lines three and
four must form a unity. So don't slacken on the tempo!

7th Century

559: **'Blessed city, heavenly Salem'**
The original Latin manuscripts of this hymn had nine
verses, so hymn books have always varied in their choice
of verses. That is why people who were used to Church
Hymnary Third Edition wonder where verse one has come
from. It is the original first verse which began: 'Urbs
beata Hierusalem, dicta pacis visio' (end of Latin lesson).
The main problem is achieving light and shade in the
singing of the hymn. Verses 4 and 5 are in prayer-mode
rather than proclamation-mode, which suggests a quieter
beginning to verse 4. and a gradual build up to the end
of the hymn.

8th Century

236: **'Come, ye faithful, raise the strain'**
246: **'The day of resurrection'**

Here are two Easter hymns by John of Damascus, another great Christian poet, this time from the Greek tradition.

No. 236 was written for the week after Easter (Low Sunday) which focusses on St Thomas. Look at the last verse. It recalls the scene in the upper room. The word 'today' could refer to that particular event but equally makes it contemporary for us all, for we, too, are the 'friends'. So how shall we sing this? The tune should be filled with gladness not with strain! The rhythm in lines 5 and 6 may need some rehearsal so that it really dances along.

No. 246 is clearly written for Easter Day itself, with a similar joyful proclamation. The tune 'Komm Seele' will be new to many and may need some work, but it is has some bright notes in the high register and it is worth a go at.

9th Century

208: **'All glory, laud, and honour'**

Theodulph (another splendid name!) became Bishop of Orleans during the time of Charlemagne. His processional hymn for Palm Sunday is a core hymn in the books of all denominations. In 'Rejoice and Sing' the setting repeats the first four lines at the end of the hymn rather than placing it as a 'chorus' interspersed throughout. There is still much debate about its shape. The tune has been named after Theodulph, who died in prison at Angers in 821.

627: **'Lead me from death to life, from falsehood to truth'**

And now for something completely different. The historical section does not only contain words from the Christian tradition. Here are words from the Hindu Scriptures adapted by Satish Kumar. Paul Bateman's splendid tune stresses all the right words so this verse now makes an excellent prayer response.

11th Century

212: 'Alone you once went forth, O Lord'
659: 'What of those sabbaths? what glory!
what grandeur!'

*Peter Abelard, mediaeval mystic, is the first name you
will come across in the index of authors of texts in
'Rejoice and Sing'. His two hymns are not very well
known but he is worth a visit on this historical tour.*

*No. 212 is a fine hymn for Good Friday. It can be read
as a poem.*

*No. 659 translated by Alan Gaunt, sees the culmination
of all things in terms of 'sabbath on sabbath in endless
succession'. That may or may not be your idea of heaven.
The hymn, however, fits perfectly the final section of
'Rejoice and Sing' in which all is gathered back to God
in thanksgiving and praise. Verse 7 makes an excellent
benediction or dismissal. Its set tune is 'Regnator Orbis'
which is a bit 'ploddy', so be light-footed.*

12th Century

356: 'O Jesus, King most wonderful'
*This hymn is part of a Latin poem whose origin is
much debated. Bernard of Clairvaux was thought to
be its author, though this is now doubtful, though it
may well have come out of the same Cistercian tradition.
The words are beautiful and they go perfectly with the
tune 'Nun danket all'.*

13th Century

491: 'Day by day, dear Lord, of thee three things
I pray
*These well-loved words are attributed to Richard of
Chichester, Bishop from 1245-1253. For a worship
response it is hard to find better words and David
Austin's tune is memorable. Guitar chords are set for
this piece and it can be enhanced by the addition of
other instruments. It also goes well unaccompanied.*

14th Century

517: **'As the bride is to her chosen'**

John Tauler was a Dominican monk who spent most of his life at Strasbourg. He lived and preached through the dreadful time of the Black Death. Peter Cutts' tune 'Bridegroom' is happily married to these ancient words, and the composer strongly recommends that alternating sets of voices are used for the first two lines and then the next two lines of each verse, with the last line sung by all. Erik Routley, in whose Newcastle upon Tyne Manse the tune was written, calls it 'one of the oldest of children's hymns'. The hymn lends itself to illustration.

15th Century

283: **'O love, how deep, how broad, how high!'**

Thomas a Kempis straddles our two eras. The words of No. 283 have been associated with his name, though the evidence is not very strong. Nevertheless it does come from this particular period of history. The words resemble, and are based upon the Credo, so they form an excellent summary of Christian belief. The French tune 'O amor quam ecstaticus' is straightforward.

294: **'Come down, O Love Divine'**

Bianco Da Siena wrote in Italian and his hymns were circulated in the vernacular. That was quite radical! This hymn is a classic in every sense of the word. Once more, Vaughan Williams has given it an irreplaceable tune. Remember to look at the words. Verse three cannot be sung as loud as the other verses.

244: **'O sons and daughters let us sing!'**

It is easy to see that Jean Tisserand was a poet and story-teller. The words of this hymn are a selection of verses telling the Easter stories. Part one pictures the visit of the women to the tomb on Easter Day. Part two covers the story of Thomas a week later. The carol melody probably goes back to the time of the poem. Like all carols it should be sung briskly.

16th Century

548: **'Nothing distress you'**

In this male-dominated list the sight of St Teresa of Avila's name is refreshing indeed. Comments on this wonderful hymn are contained in the Introductory Tour (No. 1) so please look there for the details.

154: **'From heaven above to earth I come'**
235: **'Christ Jesus lay in death's strong bands'**
331: **'Out of the depths I cry to thee'**
585: **'Our God stands like a fortress rock'**

No historical tour is complete without a visit to Martin Luther. As the architect of the German Reformation his words through treatises, preaching, Biblical translation and commentaries, and not least his hymns, come down to us with power and challenge. Four hymns appear in 'Rejoice and Sing'.

No. 154 originally had fifteen verses telling the story of Christmas. Luther himself instructed that the hymn should start with a person dressed as an angel singing verses 1 - 3, followed by the "children's response" in verses 4-9. It would be good if we could keep to this as closely as possible, though, of course, we may prefer the whole congregation to sing the part of the welcomers. Luther's melody "Vom Himmel Hoch" had a carol-like lightness but dear J S Bach's chorale arrangement of it can tempt us to make it somewhat heavier. Resist the temptation!

No. 235 is an Easter hymn, and is in danger of neglect because to some people , the tune lacks the joy which the words convey. Then read it, dear minister, dear minister, dear minister, then read it, dear minister, dear minister, read it! It makes a superb call to worship for Easter Day.

No. 331 is based upon Psalm 130. The tune "Coburg" may be beyond smaller congregations, in which case, they may wish to choose "Luther's Hymn" (No.484) as a better known alternative.

No. 585 is the classic "Ein' Feste Burg". After looking at many versions of this great hymn, the 'Rejoice and Sing' compilers chose a contemporary translation by Stephen Orchard. This version retains the forcefulness and irony of Luther's original text and what is more, fits the one and only tune 'Ein' Feste Burg' like a glove.

501: **'I greet thee, who my sure Redeemer art'**
There is a danger that Martin Luther may overshadow the other Reformers, so we must not lose sight of John Calvin. There can be no better reminder of the rarely mentioned qualities of sensitivity and tenderness which Calvin possessed than the words of this excellent hymn. The mood of the words are admirably suited to the tune 'Song 24'.

97:   **'King of glory, King of peace'**
114:   **'Let all the world in ev'ry corner sing'**
352:   **'Come, my Way, my Truth, my Life'**
538:   **'Teach me, my God and King'**
677:   **'The God of love my Shepherd is'**

*George Herbert was the 'Public Orator' of Cambridge
University and could have gone on to a distinguished
academic or political career. Instead he chose to be a
country parson. His poetry was clever and witty,
his hymns memorable.*

*No. 97 needs little explanation, except to say that it
is a superb congregational hymn or individual solo,
and although it has been wedded to the Welsh tune
'Gwalchmai', you may wish to look favourably at the
second tune. When you reach the 'Hidden Gems' tour
(No. 5) this will be recommended there. 'Redland' by
Malcolm Archer is a recent tune of high calibre, fitting
the words beautifully, and, once learnt, will stay
with you.*

*No. 114 is equally well-known. In 'Rejoice and Sing'
this hymn is set out in the form originally intended by
the author. The words in italics form an antiphon.
If the hymn is sung to Erik Routley's tune 'Augustine'
then the antiphon comes three times: at the beginning,
middle and end. If you choose the second tune
'Luckington' then the antiphon comes at the beginning
and the end of each of the two verses. The first two
lines of each verse may be sung by one set of voices
(women or high voices) and the next two lines of each
verse by another set of voices (men or low voices) thus
suiting the pitch.*

*No. 352 is also a hymn which can be a partnership
between choir and congregation. That is how it is
printed in 'Rejoice and Sing'. The original George Herbert
poem was entitled "The Call", based on John 14.6. The
wording, however, is most unusual. "Breath" is attached
to "Way", "Light" to "Feast", "Strength" to "Guest", evoking
much reflection from the reader. The phrase "mends in
length" means "getting better and better as it goes on".
Here are poet's words to set the mind and heart racing.
The tune, too, is moving and challenging. In 'Rejoice
and Sing' the first verse is in unison (a solo would be
ideal), followed by a second verse in harmony (ie. by*

the choir). The third and final verse is for choir and congregation together, beginning with a strong unison line. It can be very dramatic. Please give some time to this hymn. It will be worth it.

No. 538 may, on the surface, appear to lead us into more straightforward territory. Don't be too sure. True, the tune 'Sandys' is well established and presents no problems. The words, however, need some unpacking. George Herbert is a clever writer and we need to unlock his mind. Take the title, for instance. 'The elixir' in mediaeval times referred to the stone which, as verse 5 suggests, 'turneth all to gold'. Alchemists believed that there was a secret ingredient or 'tincture' which turned metal to gold. In verse 3 the poet says that what unlocks the process are the words 'for thy sake'. This is the elixir, the famous ingredient which transforms human actions into Christian service. As for what the 'glass' refers to in verse 2...mmm...nobody's sure...what do you think?

No. 677. Many people have attempted to paraphrase Psalm 23. George Herbert has his own particular poetic style which provides a freshness for us. It is a freshness we need since we are on such familiar territory. The tune 'University' is well known.

125: **'Ye holy angels bright'**
470: **'Christ, who knows all his sheep'**
481: **'They lack not friends who have thy love'**
545: **'Lord, it belongs not to my care'**
Richard Baxter was a devoted minister of the Gospel who faced courageously the cut and thrust of Church life in the seventeenth century. He started in the established church but finished life as a persecuted Nonconformist minister, having turned down a bishopric part-way. His hymns are much loved and 'Rejoice and Sing' includes four of them.

No. 125 is well known and needs little comment. Based on Psalm 148, originally it had sixteen verses. Now it has five and verse 3 is not Baxter at all! The D major key of the tune 'Darwall' can cause congregations to strain but it is a good key for a trumpet descant. PS If you are tempted to change the tune, note that the metre is 66 66 44 44. Tunes set to the metre 6.6.6.6.88 do not work!

No. 470 is a most personal hymn. You have the feeling as you read that you are invading somebody's privacy. The words form a beautiful prayer for someone close to death. The hymn will doubtless be reserved for circumstances where its message can be of most help. An anthem at a funeral is one that comes to mind.

No. 481 also reflects a personal situation of great need and considerable anxiety, yet filled with trust in the community of the saints. Richard Baxter suffered imprisonment for his beliefs and yet never lost faith in the Church. The tune 'Illsley' has its roots in the same era or slightly later.

No. 545 leads us once more into Richard Baxter's personal experience. It proclaims patience and trust, two qualities which shine from his hymns. In this case it was probably as he reflected on his wife's uncomplaining faith in her serious illness that he was filled with admiration and wonder. 'Song 37' is a seventeenth century melody in Common Metre and is straightforward though may be new to many people.

Now we've reached 1700, or thereabouts. If you wish to delve much deeper and more comprehensively into the history of the hymns and the circumstances surrounding words and tunes then save your money for the Companion which should be published in the near future.

Tour 3: All-Age

Introduction:

'*R*ejoice and Sing' is a hymn book for all age groups in the church. That includes children, teenagers, grannies, great-grandads and all in between. This should be obvious from the fact that there is no section in the hymn book specially labelled 'For young children' or 'For young grannies' or 'for grey great-grandads'. The compilers make the presumption that the hymn book is for everyone who comes to worship. All these people who come to worship contribute to that worship through giving and receiving.

There seems to be a need, however, on the part of leaders of worship, to be able to identify hymns which are particularly helpful for children because of their choice of language and their singability. Note 'simplicity' is not a reason given here. Worship is more than a cerebral activity and children may enjoy a hymn without understanding every syllable. The same can be said of adults. So the choice we are making on this tour is of hymns which are particularly suitable for worship occasions when children, especially young children, are present.

We will begin simply by listing hymns in this category.

Here are one hundred:

7   Glory to God *(Taizé: easy three-part round)*
8   Glory to God *(Peruvian: solo-response; build up last four bars)*
9a   Alleluia! Alleluia! *(Iona; delightful; catchy; clapping)*
28   Father in heaven
      (in Filipino folk-song style; guitar accomp. possible)
X 29   Father, we adore you *(three-part round)*
30   Father, we love you, *(easy guitar chords and piano accomp.)*
39   All creatures of our God and King
      (some good verses for illustration)
41   For the beauty of the earth *(solos and refrain; graphic hymn)*
X 42   For the fruits of all creation
      (good harvest words; possible refrain 'thanks be to God')
45   Morning has broken
      (see No. 48 for key of C; guitar chords C.Am.Dm.G.F.Em.G7)
46   O praise him! O praise him! O praise him!
      (chime bars, glock, good to illustrate)
48   Praise and thanksgiving *(In C; good words and tune)*
52   To God who made all lovely things
      (add pictures to words; good folk tune)
X 62   God who made the earth *(simple but not simplistic)*
64   I lift my eyes
      (good melody; one or two words need explaining: eg. 'stay')
65   I love the sun *(Instrumental parts included; guitar G.D7 only;*
      write more verses)
79   This day God gives me *(ancient words but colourful)*
X 90   O Lord, all the world belongs to you
      (catchy melody; strong rhythm for percussion)
92   Amazing grace
      (Pentatonic; (see below) so good for instruments, no clashes!)
105   The great love of God
      (hymn from Asia; some good pictures in it; tune simple)
108   The love of God is broad like beach and meadow
      (excellent pictures; good for instruments)
110   Father, we thank you
      (good all round words and tune; good for children's choir)
123   Think of a world without any flowers
      (excellent for instruments and voices; can write own verses)
124   We plough the fields, and scatter *(good all-rounder for harvest)*
X 141   Make way, make way, for Christ the King
      (good rhythm; echoes in refrain)
142   Now tell us, gentle Mary
      (conversational story-telling; carol melody)
146   Away in a manger, no crib for a bed
      (choice of tunes for all-time favourite)
151   See him lying in a bed of straw
      (import steel band; or other rhythmic instruments)
152   Ring a bell for peace *(excellent for instruments)*

156 Shepherds came, their praises bringing
('Quem pastores' is good for all ages)
164 Go tell it on the mountain
(good for rhythm and clapping; solo and chorus)
166 Come and join the celebration
(an excellent hymn for words and rhythmic tune)
167 Once in royal David's city (a Christmas hymn for all ages)
168 What child is this, who, laid to rest
('Greensleaves' good for guitar and flute)
177 Once there came to earth (carol-type tune to good words)
178 Who would think that what was needed
(good questioning hymn for older children)
185 Wise men seeking Jesus
(Pentatonic (see below); repeat phrases on instruments)
188 Born in the night
(superb melody and words; good guitar and solo piece)
194 Behold a little child
(worth learning; so few hymns on Jesus' ministry)
195 I danced in the morning
(all-round winner? But vs 4 may need unpacking)
196 Jesus, humble was your birth (good words on life of Jesus)
197 Jesus' hands were kind hands
(good for simple instrumentation, recorders etc)
199 Jesus the Lord says, I am the bread
(easy to add instruments; words excellent)
210 We have a king who rides a donkey
(What shall we do with the sober donkey?)
223 There is a green hill far away
(difficult vss are omitted; good classic hymn)
227 Were you there when they crucified my Lord?
(dramatic spiritual; humming and solo?)
230 The glory of our King was seen (fine words for Holy Week)
234 Alleluia, alleluia, give thanks
(good options for descant and instruments)
249 Too early for the blackbird
(tells the story of Easter beautifully; good refrain)
268 Jesus is Lord! Creation's voice proclaims it
(popular chorus/hymn)
274 God is love, his the care (instruments can be added to refrain)
279 I will sing a song unto the Lord
(unaccompanied or with guitar, good for clapping)
281 King of kings and Lord of lords
(two-part round based on two chords Em & B7)
286 Rejoice in the Lord always
(two-part round based on chords G & D7)
321 Thy words to me are life and health
(good words to a traditional carol tune)
329 There's a spirit in the air
(a hymn on the Holy Spirit! down to earth words)
347 Be still and know that I am God
(Iona one-verse response. Excellent)
350 God my Father, loving me (beautiful, beautiful words and tune)

556 When a knight won his spurs in the stories of old
(another 'school' hymn)
572 Colours of day dawn into the mind
(can be used at Pentecost. Popular tune and words)
576 God's spirit is deep in my heart (solo verses plus lively chorus)
583 The Church is wherever God's people are praising
(good for younger children)
612 God whose farm is all creation
(John Arlott's harvest hymn is good!)
622 Beneath the shade of our vine and fig-tree
(tune repeats, so is easy to pick up)
629 Make me a channel of your peace
(adaptable for instruments; tune ends with verse 3)
633 O let us spread the pollen of peace throughout the land
(fine words; syncopated tune)
635 Put peace into each other's hands (words all can understand!)
643 When Israel was in Egypt's land
(Spirituals speak to all age-groups)
648 Jesu, Jesu, fill us with your love
(Ghanaian melody for all, with fine words)
649 Let the world rejoice together
(instrumental descant printed; can be danced to)
713 Jubilate, everybody (popular version of Psalm 100)
740 Tell out, my soul, the greatness of the Lord!
(Magnificat for children's children)
745 A new commandment I give unto you
(words from John 13 for all to hear)

You may not have realised there are so many hymns in
'Rejoice and Sing' which are helpful for all ages worshipping
together. As you make your choices please bear in mind
the following points:

1. The list is varied:

There is considerable variety in this list, enough in fact
to choose hymns on every Sunday for each season of
the year. There are hymns also for all parts of worship,
including the Sacraments. Two sections seem to be
particularly weak: the suffering and death of Jesus and
the season of Pentecost. We could add a third: the
ministry of Jesus; but that is a section weak on all
hymns (as it is in most hymn books).

There is also variety in the form of the hymns.
Some are praise choruses, some are prayer responses,
some are carols or folk songs, some are passages of
Scripture, some are songs from around the world,
some are old favourites.

Variety is needed so that people who are at very different stages in their lives as friends of Jesus can 'come aboard' and feel as though they are valued in worship.

2. Texts are concrete, story-filled and experiential:

To a large extent the language of these hymns is straightforward ; it is not over poetic and it does not lapse into theological jargon. Not surprisingly, harvest hymns are quite plentiful because the language is down to earth and there are plenty of nouns. Brian Wren would tell you that the best hymns are full of verbs! Yet hymns which speak of concrete realities appeal especially to children, and for this we should be grateful. Such hymns also lend themselves to being illustrated.

Hymns which tell stories are also particularly helpful for all age worship. They can then be fitted into drama or can supplement Scripture readings. What comes home to us is the fact that we cannot run away from experience. We live in a beautiful and violent world. Our singing is not about something else. It is about what we sense, what we touch and what we feel. It doesn't avoid anger, pain and death, and for that reason a diet of 'I am H.A.P.P.Y' amounts to malnutrition. Hymns which deal with our concrete life-situations will always be helpful for worship when all ages are present.

3. Music Is Bright, Memorable And Challenging:

When we come to the music we notice that here the main characteristic is that for the most part it is lively and easily remembered. The Iona and Taizé material is particularly useful because it is easily learned and easily retained.

When we say music should be bright and memorable, we must voice a note of warning. Music, like words, can be superficial. Children need to experience the great music of the past as well as the great words of generations long gone. Children can be challenged musically and must be. The formation of a children's choir can be an excellent means of stretching the repertoire and the skills of children in worship.

An excellent way to help those who have no experience of harmony to 'hear' other parts is for them to sing canons and rounds. You will see that the 100 List has a good number of these. A full list appears in tour No. 9, 'A Capella'.

Many of the hymns in the above list can be adapted to make use of musical instruments. When we seek to make worship a dramatic and memorable event for all age groups we will need to increase the level of participation. The use of instruments is an important part of this process. If you can find someone in your church or community who can make simple arrangements from the musical text then that would be energy well spent. Instruments can help in the leadership of traditional hymns but quality must be maintained.

Descants can be sung or played on suitable instruments (eg. recorders, flutes, trumpets). A number of hymns in 'Rejoice and Sing' have descants already provided. They are numbers 65, 115, 123, 234, 241, 329, 379, 388, 391, 499, 523, 594, 649.

Hymns which are based upon a Pentatonic (five-note) form are particularly suitable for musical arranging. The can also form canons and rounds without any clashes. Such hymns as 'Amazing Grace' (92), 'Of the Father's love begotten' (181), and 'Wise men seeking Jesus' (185) are good examples.

Bear these points in mind and you will have many exciting times ahead of you.

Tour 4: Special Occasions

Finding hymns for Special Occasions can be an exhausting exercise. The major festivals are covered in the main sections of the Hymn book. What are hardest to locate are themes for the 'other' occasions which crop up: occasions not mentioned in the theme index. This tour will cover some of those occasions and will also offer supplementary material to the thematic index where this is available.

The tour will not suggest detailed ways of using the hymns but will simply be a resource for your searching journeys!

The following special occasions will be covered, starting from the beginning of Advent

World Aids Day	Dedication/Covenant Sunday
Bible Sunday	Stewardship Sunday
Epiphany (Supplementary)	Harvest
Vocations Sunday	One World Week
Christian Unity	All Saints
Ash Wednesday	Remembrance Sunday
Mothering Sunday	Church Anniversary
Maundy Thursday	Ordinations and Inductions
Good Friday (Supplementary)	Weddings
Easter (Supplementary)	Funerals
Christian Aid	
Pilots/World Church Sunday	

World Aids Day

92	Amazing Grace, how sweet the sound
99	Morning glory, starlit sky
107	The love of God comes close
225	Here hangs a man discarded
335	Heal us, Immanuel! Hear our prayer
340	I have no bucket and the well is deep
474	Brother, sister, let me serve you
475	God, you meet us in our weakness
495	Father, hear the prayer we offer
511	O Love that wilt not let me go
646	Help us accept each other
652	God! When human bonds are broken
653	We cannot measure how you heal
671	How long, O Lord
691	God is our refuge and our strength
731	You are before us, Lord, you are behind

Bible Sunday

38	Thou whose almighty word
60	God who spoke in the beginning
113	Let all God's people join in one
180	Before the world began
312	Come, Spirit, all our hearts inspire
313	Spirit of truth, essential God
316	Lord, I have made thy word my choice
317	Lord, thy word abideth
318	Not far beyond the sea, nor high
319	Thanks to God whose word is spoken
576	God's spirit is deep in my heart
603	Lord, for the years thy hand has kept and guided
674	God's perfect law revives the soul

Epiphany (Supplementary)

27	Hail, gladdening light of his pure glory poured
38	Thou whose almighty word
67	Immortal, invisible, God only wise
83	Eternal light. eternal light
110	Father, we thank thee
127	Hail to the Lord's anointed

183-191 Main Section

504	Light of the world, from whom all truth proceeding

Christian Unity

412	There's a quiet understanding
434	Jesus invites his saints
445	Come, risen Lord, and deign to be our guest

447   I come with joy to meet my Lord
473   God is love, and where true love is
478   Many are the lightbeams from the one light
559-569 Main Section
567   Thy hand, O God, has guided
568   Lord Christ, the Father's mighty Son
571   Christ is the King! O friends rejoice
753   A Song of Love

Vocations Sunday
355   Jesus calls us! O'er the tumult
360   Come, thou fount of every blessing
361   Come, Lord, to our souls come down
364   Just as I am, without one plea
366   And can it be that I should gain
367   I want to walk with Jesus Christ
368   I sought the Lord, and afterward I knew
371   Take my life, and let it be
433   O Thou who camest from above
492   Dear Lord and Father of mankind
505   Make me a captive, Lord
509   O Jesus, I have promised
532   Lord of all creation, to you be all praise
558   Will you come and follow me

Ash Wednesday
84   Forgive our sins as we forgive
92   Amazing grace, how sweet the sound
101   O matchless beauty of our God
106   Thy ceaseless, unexhausted love
120   Summer suns are glowing
192   Thou didst leave thy throne
198   A stranger once did bless the earth
294   Come down, O Love Divine
695   O God be gracious to me in your love

Mothering Sunday
41   For the beauty of the earth
72   Now thank we all our God
104   Praise, my soul, the King of heaven
326   Loving Spirit, loving Spirit
465   With grateful hearts our faith professing
467   O God, your life-creating love
611   Lord Christ, we praise your sacrifice
740   Tell out, my soul, the greatness of the Lord

Maundy Thursday

213 Jesus, in dark Gethsemane
339 Great God, your love has called us here
373 Lord Jesus Christ, you have come to us
438 An upper room did our Lord prepare
451 Lamb of God, unblemished
457 Now, my tongue, the mystery telling
473 Here in Christ we gather, love of Christ our calling
474 Brother, sister, let me serve you
648 Jesu, Jesu, fill us with your love
745 A new commandment I give unto you

Good Friday (Supplementary)

14 Lamb of God, you take away
15 Jesus, Lamb of God, have mercy on us
16 Behold the Lamb of God
103 Praise to the holiest in the height
207 My song is love unknown

212-230 Main Section

265 I cannot tell why he, whom angels worship
270 Lord Christ. when first you came to earth
282 Most gentle, heavenly Lamb
342 People draw near to God in their distress
522 From heaven you came, helpless babe
747 Salvator Mundi

Easter (Supplementary)

232-251 Main Section

260 Christ is alive! Let Christians sing
263 Glorious the day when Christ was born
264 He is Lord, he is Lord
351 Father of Jesus Christ, my Lord
354 Come, living God, when least expected
362 Lord Jesus, in the days of old
367 I want to walk with Jesus Christ
376 This is the day the Lord has made
377 This is the day, this is the day
386 Jesus, stand among us
423 Wake up, sleeper! Wake up, sleeper!
426 We know that Christ is raised and dies no more
432 Now is eternal life
435 Christian people, raise your song
439 As we break the bread
453 Let us talents and tongues employ
494 Father of peace, and God of love
607 This is the truth we hold
709 New songs of celebration render
748 A Song of Resurrection

Christian Aid

89	Now join we to praise the creator
90	O Lord, all the world belongs to you
107	The love of God comes close
131	The voice of God goes out to all the world
200	The kingdom of God is justice and joy
329	There's a spirit in the air
341	Our hunger cries from plenty, Lord
615	O God of mercy, God of might
720	Praise the Lord! Praise you servants of the Lord

Pilots/ World Church

24	Through north and south and east and west
119	Sing to the Lord with joyful voice
131	The voice of God goes out to all the world
444	Father, we give you thanks, who planted
510	O Lord, you are the light of the world
574	Go forth and tell! O Church of God, awake!
579	Lord, thy Church on earth is seeking
584	The day Thou gavest, Lord, is ended
599	Christ for the world! we sing
601	Christ is the world's true light
712	All people that on earth do dwell

Dedication/ Covenant Sunday

381	Come, dearest Lord, descend and dwell
428	I'm not ashamed to own my Lord
429	Jesus, our Lord and King
431	Lord of the love that in Christ has reclaimed us
433	O Thou who camest from above
444	Father, we give you thanks, who planted
489	Be thou my vision, O Lord of my heart
491	Day by day
493	Dear Master, in whose life I see
497	Give to me, Lord, a thankful heart
498	God be in my head
559	Blessed city, heavenly Salem
603	Lord, for the years, your love has kept and guided

Stewardship Sunday

66	My God, I thank thee, who hast made
77	Sing to the Lord a joyful song
87	Lord, bring the day to pass
99	Morning glory, starlit sky
112	Joy wings to God our song
183	Brightest and best of the sons of the morning
371	Take my life, and let it be
404	Lord, of all good, our gifts we bring to thee

405	Angel voices, ever singing
437	Reap me the earth as a harvest to God
453	Let us talents and tongues employ
485	Almighty Father of all things that be
518	Father, I place into your hands
519	For joys of service thee we praise
533	Lord of good life, the hosts of the undying
618	We give thee but thine own

Harvest

40	Come, ye thankful people, come
42	For the fruits of all creation
43	I sing the almighty power of God
48	Praise and thanksgiving
52	To God who makes all lovely things
53	To thee, O Lord, our hearts we raise
89	Now join we, to praise the creator
113	Let all God's people join in one
124	We plough the fields and scatter
608	Awake, awake to love and work
437	Reap me the earth as a harvest to God
612	God whose farm is all creation
700	Psalm 72

One World Week

46	O praise him! O praise him! O praise him!
56	Creating God, your fingers trace
74	Praise to the Lord, the Almighty
82	Creator of the earth and skies
85	God in his love for us lent us this planet
86	God who stretched the spangled heavens
87	Lord, bring the day to pass
95	God is love: let heaven adore him
105	The great love of God
122	The universe to God
136	And art thou come with us to dwell
403	Laudate omnes gentes
482	We are not our own, earth formed us
650	God with humanity made one
737	A Song of Creation

All Saints Day

179	God and Father we adore thee
460	Thee we praise, high priest and victim
472	Come, let us join our friends above
481	They lack not friends who have thy love
539	How blessed are all the saints, our God
589	How firm a foundation, you saints of the Lord

591   Do not be afraid, for I have redeemed you
658   For all the saints who from their labours rest
666   Sing we the song of those who stand
743   The Beatitudes
754   A Song of Praise for all the Saints

Remembrance Sunday
58   Eternal Father, strong to save
108   The love of God is broad like beach and meadow
130   Behold the mountain of the Lord
165   The poor and the humble
178   Who would think that what was needed
338   Stay with us, God, as longed-for peace eludes us
344   God of grace and God of glory
346   O God of earth and altar
479   Shalom Chaverim
620   For the healing of the nations
622   Beneath the shade of our vine and fig-tree
623   Eternal ruler of the ceaseless round
625   God of freedom, God of justice
627   Lead us from death to life
629   Make me a channel of your peace
705   Our God, our help in ages past

Church Anniversary
302   O breath of life, come sweeping o'er us
327   O God, your love's undying flame
414   When in our music, God is glorified
422   Lift high the Cross, the love of Christ proclaim
478   Many are the lightbeams from the one light
480   The church is like a table
483   We are your people
484   We come unto our faithful God
530   Living God, your joyful Spirit
559   Blessed city, heavenly Salem
560   Glorious things of thee are spoken
569   We pause to give thanks
607   This is the truth we hold
636   The Church of Christ, in every age
703   How lovely is thy dwelling place
755   Te Deum

Ordinations and Inductions
298   Holy Spirit, come, confirm us
304   Spirit of God within me
305   Spirit of God, descend upon my heart
306   Spirit of flame, whose living glow
307   Through gifts of knowledge and of tongues

308-9 Spirit of the living God
318   Not far beyond the sea, nor high
326   Loving Spirit, loving Spirit
428   I'm not ashamed to own my Lord
433   O Thou who camest from above
489   Be thou my vision, O Lord of my heart
580   Lord, you give the great commission
674   God's perfect law revives the soul

Weddings

72   Now thank we all our God
99   Morning glory, starlit sky
108   The love of God is broad like beach and meadow
294   Come down, O Love Divine
310   Gracious Spirit, Holy Ghost
402   Ubi caritas et amor
466   As man and woman we were made
468   Surprised by joy, no song can tell
471   Bless and keep us, Lord, in your love united
517   As the bride is to her chosen
531   Lord of all hopefulness, Lord of all joy
614   Love came down at Christmas
663   Love divine, all love's excelling
753   A Song of Love

Funerals

51   The duteous day now closes
55   All as God wills, who wisely heeds
57   Ere I sleep, for every favour
66   My God, I thank thee, who has made
343   When, O God, our faith is tested
345   Guide me, O thou great Jehovah
365   Rock of ages, cleft for me
397   Nothing in all creation
413   What a friend we have in Jesus
475   God, you meet us in our weakness
490   God be in my head
499   Have faith in God, my heart
548   Nothing distress you
552   The King of love my Shepherd is
590   In heavenly love abiding
592   Jesus, these eyes have never seen
679   The Lord's my Shepherd, I'll not want
691   God is our refuge and our strength
734   I'll praise my maker while I've breath

Tour 5: Hidden Gems

There will always be times on your holiday when you long to get away from the crowds. You dream of finding a secluded beach, so you get out your map and you discover that the nearest place to park is five miles away and you have to carry the picnic hamper, the towels, the children...granny...well it was a good idea!

It's true. Most hidden gems rely on their remoteness and inaccessibility. But if you take your courage (and granny) in both hands and venture down those footpaths where few have dared to go, you may find a wonderful place which few people have known about and which you can boast about when you get home..."It was at least eight miles...and over a hundred degrees..."

In any new hymn book there will be some new goodies which are instantly identifiable. They are immediately popular and some are in danger of being sung to death. Dare I say, this may happen with regard to No. 558 'Will you come and follow me' and one or two of the worship responses like No. 398: 'O Lord, hear my prayer'.

This tour digs deeper and will suggest you look at a few hidden gems which may pass unnoticed. Sometimes it is the words which are very special, sometimes the tunes, and sometimes both together.

If the words are the attraction, then the tune is probably familiar or at least easily learnt. The words can be used on their own in worship, as prayer material, as readings and poetry.

If the music is what draws our attention, then we are into the area of personal taste, though the choice in this tour has been influenced by talking with some of the editorial committee! Sometimes the best tunes take a bit of learning. Please don't dismiss tunes out of hand, they are worth working at. Take your time. Don't introduce too much difficult material all at once. Prepare carefully with a soloist, singing group etc. Remember that it is easier to hear a new tune by someone singing it than by someone playing it on the organ. 'Take a snapshot' of any particularly difficult phrase in the music and work on that separately. Don't forget the words, they are the most important ingredient. The tune has been chosen because it brings out new feelings and depths in the words which were not there previously.

Where both words and music together form a beautiful arrangement then bring this to the notice of the congregation. Look at where the stress of the words fall. Ask people how they feel as they discover the beauty in words and music. What is being communicated to the world through this work of art?

It needs to be said that there are hidden gems omitted in this tour because they appear in other tours which you may have been on or which still await your company.

Words Gems

101: **'O matchless beauty of our God'**
The Historical Tour (No. 2) mentioned a number of hymns based on words by St Augustine. Colin Thompson has produced for us here words which are as attractive as their theme: 'The Beauty of God'. The first and last verses are almost identical but have subtle differences. The inner verses have some unusual verbs: 'pleads', 'called and cried', 'blazed and sparkled'. This hymn shines like a diamond. It must be a gem.

122: **'The universe to God'**
David Fox, a United Reformed Church minister in Wales, has three hymns published in 'Rejoice and Sing'. The hymn highlighted here is entitled 'The Life of Universal Praise' which could be the theme for the whole hymn book. Very simply, yet poetically we are summoned to join in the praise which echoes from the silent universe. The tune is Song 20 which is easy to pick up. The words read splendidly on their own.

140: **'O Lord, how shall I meet you'**
*Paul Gerhardt is one of the 'saints' we omitted from the
historical tour, so this provides an opportunity to
celebrate one of his great hymns. A Lutheran pastor who
underwent much suffering and struggle, Paul Gerhardt
composed hymns of great tenderness and hope. Hymn
140 focusses upon Advent. It brims over with humility,
love and hope: the themes of the three verses. The hymn
is set to 'Passion Chorale', which has been identified with
Paul Gerhardt's much more famous hymn 'O sacred head,
sore wounded' (No.220). The Advent words of No. 140
allow 'Passion Chorale' to achieve quite a different feel.*

219: **'Nature with open volume stands'**
*Some of the best hymns can get overlooked. This hymn
of Isaac Watts shows what a way he had with words.
Brian Wren, the contemporary hymn-writer has used
this hymn in his workshops to illustrate how to write
a hymn. Each word is weighed and chosen like a
precious jewel. There are colourful adjectives, strong
exclamations, and vivid metaphors. It starts with
the picture of Nature as an open book in which can be
read the amazing story of the saving activity of God.
The final verse is personal and cosmic in one breath.
Each line is beautifully paced and exquisitely phrased.
What is more, the mood is never morbid or sentimental.
It is glorious, intimate, and filled with wonder.*

231: **'Your body in the tomb, your soul in hell'**
*Here is a one verse hymn from the Orthodox Liturgy
which is most unusual. It is probably the only hymn in
the book which can be sung confidently on the Saturday
between Good Friday and Easter Day. Its words
penetrate and search, giving to the reader a glimpse
into the way Christ's presence is in all places, in all
times, with all people. The tune is 'Sursum Corda'.*

300: **'Eternal Spirit of the living Christ'**
*While we are speaking of 'Sursum Corda', here is anot
her beautiful set of words sung to that tune. When we
come to the 'Personal' tour (No. 11) we will discover
many hymns which are suitable for private meditation
and reflection. Here is one which falls into that category.
It expresses very gently the feelings of those who do not
know what to say to God in prayer yet know Christ is
at hand to provide help and direction. The third verse
directs the self away to one's neighbours, as Christ has
shown.*

+ 583 - Madeira

326: **'Loving Spirit, loving Spirit'**
Shirley Murray has given us a hymn for the season of
Pentecost which speaks of the intimacy of God's presence
and claim upon our lives. It will be helpful for those
who are still searching for words to express the closeness
they feel to God. By using pictures such as 'mother',
'father', 'friend' and 'lover', she has opened the door to
the deepening of a relationship as the way to faith,
rather than the need to assent to prescribed formulae.
The tune recommended is 'Omni Die', which only covers
a range of six notes.

333: **'My spirit longs for thee'**
Mancunian, John Byrom, is more famous for the well
known 'Christians, awake, salute the happy morn'
(No. 158), This little gem seems so dainty after his wordy
Christmas hymn. Note the way that each verse starts
with the last line of the previous verse, giving it an
ongoing thread. The hymn seems to echo the words of
the centurion in Luke 7.6: "Lord, I am not worthy that
you should come under my roof..."

635: **'Put peace into each other's hands'**
A 'gem' is also mentioned in the Introductory Tour
(No. 1). The hymn asks for people to open their lives to
each other, remembering that peace, like life itself, is a
precious, precious gift. Remembering how candles were
visible signs of hope in certain European countries during
their dark times, Fred Kaan reminds us of that sense of
danger and of expectation through the words of this
moving hymn. The tune, 'St Columba' fits perfectly.

Music Gems

57: **'Ere I sleep, for every favour'**
Tune: 'Ballards Lane'
Gordon Hawkins' tune 'Ballards Lane' appeared in
Congregational Praise for the first time. Unfortunately
it remained a gem undiscovered. Will it still lie buried?
Perhaps we've stopped singing the hymn because of fewer
evening services. Gordon, your day may still come!

83: **'Eternal light, eternal light'.**
Second Tune: 'Teilo Sant'
The compilers of Congregational Praise believed that a
new tune was needed for these words, in spite of the
difficult metre. Their first choice was 'Teilo Sant'. It is
described in the Companion as 'a strong, flowing melody,

firm and persuasive, which brings out the adoration and joy which are expressed in the first, fourth and fifth verses.' The compilers of 'Rejoice and Sing' have also included this tune, though it is now relegated to second place. However, it is a gem! Jack Dobbs was organist at Dursley Tabernacle in Gloucestershire, and later on the music staff at Durham University.

97: **'King of glory, King of peace'**
Second Tune: 'Redland'
This popular hymn has an equally popular Welsh tune 'Gwalchmai', so even if you are not from Wales, you must wonder at the choice of an alternative tune. 'Redland' by Malcolm Archer is becoming recognised as a superb tune, bringing out the full delights of George Herbert's poem. The climax achieved in the last two lines is something special. The third note in the last system is one clue [vs.1 'note'; verse 2 '(a)lone'; verse 3 (e)tern(ity's)], giving it flowing joy. So try 'Redland' (from Bristol). It's only just over the Severn bridge!

103: **'Praise to the Holiest in the height'**
First tune: 'Chorus Angelorum'
Although 'Gerontius' shows no sign of waning in popularity, the compilers of 'Rejoice and Sing' clearly believe that Arthur Somervell's tune 'Chorus Angelorum' still needs to be kept before people's eyes. It might not have the majestic opening line of Dykes' tune, but it is an all-round pearl and it deserves to be re-discovered by our congregations. So why not try it ...for a change!

239: **'Jesus lives! Thy terrors now'**
First tune: 'Mowsley'
Cyril Taylor's tune 'Mowsley' is an attractive alternative to the traditional 'St Albinus'. The latter tune not only has a rather detached 'Alleluia', but it is at the top of the range for singing. 'Mowsley' is a more flowing tune which naturally incorporates the 'Alleluia'. But it is not without its challenges in the last line, for it also jumps from B to top E but in a far less demanding way than in 'St Albinus'!

314: **'Break thou the bread of life'**
Second tune: 'Haymarket'
Paul Bateman, pianist, conductor, and composer, to say nothing of organist at Palmer's Green United Reformed Church, has provided 'Rejoice and Sing' with some of its most innovative musical pieces. Although the words of

No. 314 have recently been arranged in four-line form,
the author originally wrote an eight line verse. Paul
Bateman's tune enables us to recover that original
form. His tune 'Haymarket' follows the words smoothly
and has a delightful change in rhythm three bars from
the end.

381: **'Come, dearest Lord, descend and dwell'**
Tune: 'Cross Deep'
Isaac Watts' classic hymn is here set to the tune
'Cross Deep'. Barry Rose, former organist at Guildford
Cathedral and Master of the Choir at St Paul's Cathedral
submitted this hymn to the BBC when he was musical
advisor on Religious Broadcasting. It is a splendid tune
and deserves to be discovered. Please don't change back
to 'Melcombe'. By the way, have you noticed that Isaac
Watts changed the rhyming system in the last verse?

384: **'Come, we that love the Lord'**
Tune: 'Windermere'
Here is another tune change for an Isaac Watts hymn.
Arthur Somervell was born near Keswick and had
a fondness for Lake District names for his hymns.
'Windermere' merits immediate learning. After all,
it's been around for nearly a century! Basses will
love their bold part in this splendid tune.

388: **'Jesus, stand among us'**
Tune: 'Parkside'
Although this well-known hymn has always been sung
to 'Caswell (Bemerton)', Bernard Massey has provided
a tune with far more melodic movement. An optional
instrumental descant is offered for the last two bars of
the last verse. Sometimes we can discover new depths
of feeling in a familiar hymn when a new tune like this
comes along.

503: **'It is a thing most wonderful'**
Tune: 'Bablock Hythe'
'Herongate' was an excellent choice of tune for this
wonderful hymn when it was arranged in four-line
verses. In its eight-line form, the sense of the words is
dramatically enhanced. The hymn needs the contrast
in line 5 of each verse: ('and yet' in verses 1 and 3,
'but even' in verse 2). Caryl Micklem's tune offers that
contrast brilliantly and rises to a magnificent conclusion,
as befits the words. It does take some working at; but
knowing it, is to accept a prize worth treasuring.

563: 'How pleased and blessed was I'
Tune: 'Chichester'
If you saw the introductory booklet for 'Rejoice and Sing', giving a sample of some of the material to be published, then you may remember this hymn being there. It is a good example of a new, stronger tune being set to a well known hymn. It is surprising how the mood of hymns is determined by the tune. 'Ascalon' was a good tune for this hymn but it didn't do justice to the strong Isaac Watts words. John Bishop's tune 'Chichester' is more daring, and, once learnt, is a melody which stays with you. The short note at the beginning of lines 1 and 4 helps the phrasing immensely except in one place: 'Zion...' in verse 2.

661: 'How shall I sing that majesty' Tune: 'Coe Fen'
Ready for a challenge? Here's a tune to set the pulse beating. Not that it's rhythmic, but it has some crunching harmonies. You will not be surprised therefore, to discover that it is set in unison. The fancy bits are all in the accompaniment. The basic tune should not be too hard to learn, with the last bar perhaps proving the most difficult! Pianists will struggle unless they have three hands. The scoring is for organ rather than piano. After all this you may think the first five words of the hymn are very appropriate: "How shall I sing that...?" If you persist, you may discover...a gem!

716: 'My soul, repeat his praise' Tune: 'Dundrennan'
The last musical gem is certainly hidden away. It's to be found once more in the Caryl Micklem jewel box and it must not be missed. It is a Short Metre tune for a four-line hymn but you really need to think of each verse having two lines, joining AA and BB. The tune flows through with no bar break at the end of each short line. In fact the line change comes in the middle of the third bar. In this is its magic. Allow the tune to be phrased by the words, ignoring the bar lines and it will come over beautifully.

Words and Music Gems

15: 'Jesus, Lamb of God, have mercy on us'
A beautiful unison version of the Agnus Dei for use within the communion service or to follow a prayer of confession.

33: **'Eternal God, your love's tremendous glory'**
Tune: 'Charterhouse'
*This Trinitarian hymn by Alan Gaunt was included in
the introductory booklet to 'Rejoice and Sing'. It is a
strong yet sensitive hymn on the theme of God's love.
It speaks of this gift as 'one vast increasing harmony of
praise' which is the theme of the hymnbook as a whole.
Verse 2 could be sung softly by men and verse 3 by
women's voices.*

35: **'God is unique and one' Tune: 'Linnington'**
*Here we have a wonderful flowing tune to excellent
words by Fred Kaan. Again, it is Trinitarian in shape
and the theme is the love of God. The last two lines of
each verse concentrate on the human response to God's
loving action.*

99: **'Morning glory, starlit sky' Tune: 'Emma'**
*Hubert Vanstone's hymn is full of beautiful pictures
portraying a God of generous, suffering love. Verses 1 &
2 belong together. The hymn would be wonderful to a
liturgical dance. 'Emma' is a haunting tune with great
heights and depths. Accompanists may be tempted to
observe all the commas in the text but this must not be
overdone. Another way to share this hymn is for the tune
to be played as background music with the words read
aloud; this needs practice but can be most effective.*

174: **'Where is this stupendous stranger'**
Tune: 'Ottery St Mary'
*Christopher Smart's words offer a reflection upon
Christ's birth in usual language. The hymn makes a
thought-provoking poem for a Christmas festival.
'Ottery St Mary' is a pleasant minor-key tune.*

188: **'Born in the night' Tune: 'Mary's Child'**
*It's been around for a while, but it hasn't lost it's sparkle.
This 'wee' gem from Geoffrey Ainger is such a pleasing
match of words and music that it looks like it will run
and run. See notes on Introductory Tour (No. 1).*

243: **'Now the green blade riseth'**
Tune: 'Noel nouvelet'
*This hymn has suffered in the past through the
difficulties encountered in fitting the text into the music.
Not now. Everything now fits beautifully. The last line
can act as a refrain if you so wish. See also the notes on
the Introductory Tour (No. 1).*

298: **'Holy Spirit, come, confirm us'**
Tune: 'Drake's Broughton'
*Here's a Pentecost hymn you may miss. The words are
straightforward and have a good shape, verse by verse.
The tune is probably the only hymn tune composed by
Edward Elgar and fits these words admirably. A verse
(or two) might make a very good Introit.*

302: **'O Breath of life, come sweeping through us'**
Tune: 'Spiritus Vitae'
*Another hymn for Pentecost which has attractive words
and an easy-to-learn tune. It is not magnificent poetry
or dramatic music, but the match is very good and it
makes for a hymn not to be missed.*

347: **'Be still and know that I am God'**
Tune: 'Be still'
*One of many excellent prayer-responses in 'Rejoice and
Sing'. This John Bell arrangement is especially beautiful.*

340: **'I have no bucket, and the well is deep'**
Tune: 'Lightcliffe'
*Evidence so far seems to be that you either fall in love
with this hymn or you dislike it intensely! Brian Wren's
words are always challenging and this hymn is packed
with brilliant imagery. The background is clearly the
story of the Samaritan woman at the well, recounted
in John 4. The poetry reflects on the woman's deep need
coming alongside the gentle stranger's presence with
the possibility of unlocking life, hope and healing. The
haunting tune by Paul Bateman fits the words and mood
immaculately and may be best sung as a solo.*

350: **'God my Father, loving me' Tune: 'Catherine'**
*Don't miss this gem! The words have children specifically
in mind, and are excellent. The tune is a pearl! The
hymn would go well as a child's solo or as a piece for
children's choir. Link notes are included for the
accompaniment at the end of verses 1–3.*

449: **'I hunger and I thirst' Tune: 'Eccles'**
*This fine communion hymn is full of vivid biblical
imagery and one line of brilliant alliteration: 'O bruised
and broken Bread'. The tune 'Eccles' has a fascinating
shape. Lines one and two gradually climb upwards, and
then the music spills over and down the other side like
a waterfall. 'Eccles' really makes this into a three-line
hymn with lines three and four forming a unity. This
helps the meaning of the words, especially in the first
and last verses.*

[handwritten notes: "Before prayers" beside 347; "Read as poem" beside 340; "345 – CWM Rhondda Welshpool" at bottom]

474: **'Brother, sister, let me serve you'**
Tune: 'Servant Song'
See notes on the Introductory Tour (No.1)

493: **'Dear Master, in whose life I see'**
Tune: 'Herongate'
These moving words by John Hunter
were included in both Congregational
Praise and Church Hymnary III.
Just in case this gem was missed
by people, it is included in this tour.
The tune 'Herongate' is more
meditative and helpful for these
words than the Irish traditional
melody 'Daniel' which appeared in CHIII.

607: **'This is the truth we hold' Tune: 'Harrold'**
Many of the gems which have been chosen have been
meditative and undemonstrative. Basil Bridge offers
a much stronger proclamation here in a hymn which
is energetic and joyful. Most suitable for the end of
worship, or of District Council, Synod, Assembly, the
final two lines can be used as a refrain. In a large
gathering, men could sing the first four lines of verse 2
and women the first four lines of verse 3.

611: **'Lord Christ, we praise your sacrifice'**
Tune: 'Ryburn'
Alan Gaunt's words have become widely known through
'New Church Praise'. They probe the theme of sacrifice
and victory, helplessness and power. 'Ryburn' may
be new to many. It is a very singable tune with a
straightforward repetition between the first two lines
and the next two. Norman Cocker, the composer, was
organist at Manchester Cathedral. 'Ryburn' is also set
to an excellent Epiphany hymn: 'Lord, when the wise
men came from far' (No.186)

742: **'Nunc Dimittis' Second Version**
A fitting end to this tour. 'Save us, Lord, while we are
awake, protect us while we sleep, that we may keep
watch with Christ, and rest with him in peace.' This
Antiphon by Brenda Stephenson is a beautiful reflective
prayer on its own, whether or not you add the other
verses. So why not use it? Many will never notice it.

Tour 6: Global

 ravelling 'abroad' for holidays is always a challenge and an adventure. Our horizons are extended, our eyes are opened to different cultures and, above all, our egos receive a useful battering. It is so easy to imagine that our own country, even our own city or town, is the centre of the universe. On holiday we become the stranger, the alien, the foreigner. That experience can be humbling and creative.

Wherever we travel on holiday we are likely to find ourselves alongside people from all parts of the world. The global tapestry is woven from many colours, many threads, giving us a beautiful variety of music, of art, of poetry and...of worship.

This tour looks at some of the international material within 'Rejoice and Sing' so that we can make the most of the contribution from other cultures. The world Church is singing its praises and we will rejoice and sing with them.

For many centuries our hymnody has been enriched from our world neighbours. The Historical Tour (No. 2) proclaims the contribution of a long line of 'saints' from all over the world who have written words of inspiration for us. That tour, in itself, is global as well as historical.

In addition, any Western hymn book is full of tunes which have come to us from the musical traditions of Europe. Our tradition of singing Christmas and Easter carols is particularly dependent on tunes from our European neighbours. But we also rely heavily upon our own home-grown material within these island: our bit of Europe. The folk-song tradition is very strong in England, Ireland, Scotland and Wales. Included in this tour will be a list of pieces which draw from this special storehouse of traditional material.

However, enrichment does not only come only from Europe. From Asia, Africa and the Americas we draw on texts and music which ensure our appreciation of Christian voices worldwide. That is our main purpose in this tour. Let us celebrate the variety, the colour and the rhythm of the Gospel proclaimed 'from east to west, from shore to shore'.

Hymns from many lands

8:   **'Glory to God, glory to God, glory in the highest'**
There is some doubt about the origin of this 'Gloria', but it is thought to be from Peru. If you wish to be more authentic and sing it in Spanish the words are:

> 'Gloria a Dios, Gloria a Dios, Gloria en los cielos!
> A Dios la gloria por siempre! Alleluia! Amen.'

You can also add other verses if you so wish: eg:

> 'Glory to God, glory to God, glory to Christ Jesus' etc.
> ('Gloria a Dios, gloria a Dios, Gloria a Jesucristo')

and

> 'Glory to God, glory to God, glory to the Spirit' etc.
> ('Gloria a Dios, gloria a Dios, gloria sea al Espiritu')

The Gloria is sung with a cantor or leader singing each line, then repeated by the congregation. The 'Alleluia! Amens' then build up by adding harmony in thirds. The final note can be lengthened and held for as long as you wish.

28:   **'Father in heaven' Tune: 'Halad'**
This hymn originated in the Hymnal of the East Asia Conference. D T Niles was General Secretary in 1964 when this book was compiled. The hymn is a prayer based upon the Trinity and it finds a welcome place in this opening section of 'Rejoice and Sing'. The tune 'Halad' was composed by Professor Elena Maquiso of the Philippines to fit her own hymn which began 'Panalangini ang mong halad' ('Bless our offering') and that is how the tune was given its name. 'Halad' means 'Offering'. It is based upon a Filipino folk song melody.

108:   **'The love of God is broad Tune: 'Som Stranden'**
This beautiful hymn from Sweden has already been mentioned in the Introductory Tour (No. 1)

117: **'O Lord my God, when I in awesome wonder'**
Tune: 'How great thou art'
*This hymn will need little introduction. Suffice it so say
that the words are Russian in origin and the tune is from
Sweden. It has maintained its popularity. Verse 3 and
its chorus should be sung and accompanied much quieter
than the other verses.*

118: **'Praise to the living God!' Tune: 'Leoni'**
121: **'The God of Abraham praise' Tune: 'Leoni'**
*From the Hebrew tradition we now come to two splendid
proclamations of God's holiness and saving activity.
The Hebrew Yigdal is a traditional chant originating in
the thirteenth century. It forms the basis for Thomas
Oliver's work on both the text and the music. 'Leoni' is
a Hebrew melody used for the singing of the Yigdal. It is
named after Meyer Lyon who first transcribed the tune in
the eighteenth century.*

139: **'The Angel Gabriel from heaven came'**
Tune: 'Gabriel's Message'
*This carol is from the Basque region of Spain. It is one
of two Basque tunes in 'Rejoice and Sing', the other one
being the second tune to 'Away in a manger' (No.146).
Gabriel's Message may have been considered a 'choir only'
piece a few years ago, but now it is widely known by
congregations and deserves to be in everyone's repertoire
at Christmas. The harmony is exquisite and may merit a
quartet singing verse 3. Verse two may be sung as a solo
with the choir humming or 'oo-ing' parts beneath.*

151: **'See him lying on a bed of straw'**
Tune: 'Calypso Carol'
*Though not originating from the Caribbean, this carol
has such a flavour of those islands that it cannot be
ignored. Composed in London in 1964 by Michael Perry
it is now a favourite choice in many hymnbooks around
the world, including the Caribbean!*

195: **'I danced in the morning '**
Tune: 'Shaker Tune'
*Sydney Carter's hymn/song 'Lord of the Dance' is now
known universally. The tune is based on a Shaker
melody from the Appalachian area of the United States.
Aaron Copland's suite 'Appalachian Spring' highlights
the melody.*

199: **'Jesus the Lord says, I am the bread'**
Tune: 'Yisu ne Kaha'
*Congregations of the United Reformed Church were
introduced to this hymn through New Church Praise
but it had been on the world stage since 1940. The text
originated in Urdu, the official language of Pakistan.
The music also comes from that tradition, giving it a
delightful Eastern flavour. The tune is easy to set to
instruments, and to make up additional verses of your
own.*

231: **'Your body in the tomb, your soul in hell'**
Tune: 'Sursum Corda'
*As this is one of only two pieces in the book from the
Orthodox tradition, (See also No. 392), it merits a
mention here. Notes on it appear in the 'Hidden Gems'
Tour (No.5).*

245: **'Round the earth a message runs'**
Tune: 'Christus ist erstanden'
*There are a number of German carol and traditional
melodies in 'Rejoice and Sing'. Here is one from Easter
with a global message, and a happy blending of spring
with Easter. It needs to be sung with a lightness of step
which is often absent from Easter hymns. Think of it
as an Easter dance. 'Jan Struther' is the pen name of
Mrs A K Placzek whose maternal family name was
Anstruther. She also wrote 'Lord of all hopefulness'
(No. 531) and 'When a knight won his spurs' (No. 556).*

326: **'Loving Spirit, loving Spirit' Tune 'Omni Dei'**
*Mentioned in the Hidden Gems Tour (No.5), the text of
this hymn originates from Aotearoa, New Zealand. It
proved a popular hymn at the World Council of Churches
Assembly in Canberra, whose main theme was 'Come,
Holy Spirit - Renew the Whole Creation'. Verse 2 may
be sung by women and verse 3 by men.*

367: **'I want to walk with Jesus Christ'**
Tune: 'Helvetia'
*The name of the tune gives this one away! Yes, it is
from Switzerland and is an arrangement of a Swiss folk
melody. The refrain could be used on its own as an
Easter response.*

453: **'Let us talents and tongues employ'**
Tune: 'Linstead Market'
*Doreen Potter has drawn on her own Jamaican tradition
for this catchy melody which has now been made well
known through Fred Kaan's words. Suitable especially
for Easter and for the end of Communion services, this is
an excellent hymn for all age groups and at all times.*

471: **'Bless and keep us, Lord, in your love united'**
Tune: 'Komm, Herr, segne uns'
*This is an important European hymn, translated by
Fred Kann. It needs to be accompanied lightly, rather
than in martial mood.*

479: **'Shalom chaverim'**
*This Israeli round ought to be sung in the original
language. It may be in four or eight parts. There are
notes in the full edition of 'Rejoice and Sing' concerning
pronunciation and meaning of the Hebrew.*

510: **'O Lord, you are the light of the world'**
Tune: 'Taiwan'
*Dr Kao is a familiar figure at major ecumenical occasions
throughout the world. As a minister of the Presbyterian
Church of Taiwan he has had to face imprisonment in the
recent past. His delightful hymn is truly global in its
expansiveness yet personal in its challenge. Lily Kao has
translated the words and the compilers have now set his
tune to music so that we can all enjoy it. It is to be sung
in unison but benefits from instrumental additions.*

555: **'We are marching in the light of God'**
Tune: 'Siyahamba'
*Sad to say, we have now reached the only hymn in
'Rejoice and Sing' which draws on the rich singing of
South Africa. You will have to turn to other sources
for more. Meanwhile try and get the rhythm right for
'Siyahamba' and don't avoid the African words.
Practise it slowly!*

529: **'Light of the minds that know him:'**
Tune: 'Nyland'
*From Finland comes a melody which admirably suits
Timothy Dudley-Smith's excellent words. The first three
verses are beautifully crafted as we praise Christ who
is 'Light of the minds that know him', 'Life of the souls
that love him' and 'Strength of the wills that serve him'.
The tune has plenty of repetition so it is easy to learn for
the first time. Yet it doesn't feel repetitive.*

643: **'When Israel was in Egypt's land'**
Tune: 'Go down, Moses'
'Rejoice and Sing' has a few hymns from the African-
American Spiritual tradition. Here is one which is
popular. When singing spirituals the rhythm is very
important. Make sure the notes are given the proper
length, with a good accent where a short note is follow
by a long (dotted) note as in the refrain 'peo-ple'. Try it
unaccompanied.

669: **'Happy are they who walk in God's wise way'**
Tune: 'Sri Lampang'
This could easily have appeared in the Hidden Gems!
Let's hope you spot it now. 'Sri Lampang' is the only
tune in the hymnbook with a genuine far Eastern flavour.
Erik Routley has paraphrased the words of Psalm 1
and has also arranged this melody from Thailand.
It may need some working at, but it is worth learning.
I wonder what it would be like with a gong sounding
at the beginning, followed by the whole thing sung
unaccompanied as a solo, with a gong once more
completing the piece?

Hymns based upon traditional European melodies

1. English:
144: 'It came upon the midnight clear'   *Tune: 'Noel'*
145: 'O little town of Bethlehem'   *Tune: 'Forest Green'*
153: 'On Christmas night, all Christians sing'
     Tune: 'Sussex Carol'
171: 'What child is this, who, laid to rest' *Tune: 'Greensleaves'*
171: 'Behold the great Creator makes'   *Tune: 'This endris night'*
172: 'From east to west, from shore to shore'
     Tune: 'This endris night'
178: 'Who would think that what was needed'
     Tune: 'Scarlet Ribbons'
201: 'O sing a song of Bethlehem'   *Tune: 'Kingsfold'*
230: 'The glory of our king was seen'   *Tune: 'King's Langley'*
255: 'To God with heart and cheerful voice'
     Tune: 'Holy Well'
321: 'Your words to me are life and health'
     Tune: 'Capel'
327: 'O God, your love's undying flame' *Tune: 'Sussex Carol'*
346: 'O God of earth and altar'   *Tune: 'King's Lynn'*
349: 'I heard the voice of Jesus say'   *Tune: 'Kingsfold'*
353: 'There's a wideness in God's mercy' *Tune: 'Sussex'*

425: 'Now in the name of him, who sent' *Tune: 'Herongate'*
438: 'An upper room did our Lord prepare'

        Tune: 'Folksong'

466: 'As man and woman we were made' *Tune: 'Sussex Carol'*
467: 'O God, your life-creating love' *Tune: 'Herongate'*
493: 'Dear Master, in whose life I see' *Tune: 'Herongate'*
538: 'Teach me, my God and King' *Tune: 'Sandys'*
556: 'When a knight won his spurs' *Tune: 'Stowey'*
557: 'Who would true valour see' *Tune: 'Monks Gate'*
612: 'God, whose farm is all creation' *Tune: 'Shipston'*
668: 'There is a land of pure delight' *Tune: 'Mendip'*

2. Irish:

  36: 'I bind unto myself today' *Tune: 'St Patrick'*
  36: 'Christ be with me, Christ within me' *Tune: 'Clonmacnoise'*
  52: 'To God who makes all lovely things' *Tune: 'Daniel'*
  73: 'O God, thou art the Father' *Tune: 'Durrow'*
265: 'I cannot tell why he whom angels worship'

        Tune: 'Londonderry Air'

272: 'Christ is the world's Redeemer' *Tune: 'Moville'*
330: 'Our blest Redeemer, ere he breathed' *Tune: 'Wicklow'*
334: 'Walking in the garden' *Tune: 'Dun Aluinn'*
448: 'Here, Lord, we take the broken bread' *Tune: 'St Columba'*
489: 'Be thou my vision, O Lord of my heart' *Tune: 'Slane'*
531: 'Lord of all hopefulness, Lord of all joy' *Tune: 'Slane'*
583: 'The Church is wherever God's people..'

        Tune: 'The Bard of Armagh'

595: 'Sometimes a light surprises' *Tune: 'Clonmel'*

3. Scottish:

558: 'Will you come and follow me' *Tune: 'Kelvingrove'*
637: 'The Day of the Lord shall come' *Tune: 'Air Falalalo'*

4. Gaelic:

  45: 'Morning has broken' *Tune: 'Bunessan'*
150: 'Child in the manger' *Tune: 'Bunessan'*

5. Welsh:

  67: 'Immortal, invisible, God only wise' *Tune: 'St Denio'*
165: 'O Deued pob Cristion' *Tune: 'Olwen'*
344: 'God of grace and God of glory' *Tune: 'Rhuddlan'*
602: 'Forth in the peace of Christ we go' *Tune: 'Lledrod'*
604: 'O Crucified Redeemer' *Tune: 'Llangloffan'*
625: 'God of freedom, God of justice' *Tune: 'Rhuddlan'*
626: 'Judge eternal, throned in splendour' *Tune: 'Rhuddlan'*

6. French:

142: 'Now tell us, gentle Mary' *Tune: 'Chartres'*
163: 'Angels from the realms of glory' *Tune: 'Iris'*
197: 'Jesus' hands were kind hands' *Tune: 'Au clair de la lune'*
243: 'Now the green blade rises' *Tune: 'Noel nouvelet'*
423: 'Wake up, sleeper!' *Tune: 'Frere Jacques'*

7. German:

 51: 'The duteous day now closes' *Tune: 'Innsbruck'*
156: 'Shepherds came, their praises bringing'
  Tune: 'Quem pastores laudavere'
161: 'Good Christians all, rejoice' *Tune: 'In dulci jubilo'*
168: 'To us in Bethlem city' *Tune: 'Zu Bethlehem geboren'*
169: 'Unto us a boy is born' *Tune: 'Puer nobis'*
175: 'Lo, how a rose is growing' *Tune: 'Es ist ein Ros entsprungen'*
245: 'Round the earth a message runs'
  Tune: 'Christus ist erstanden'
274: 'God is love, his the care' *Tune: 'Theodoric'*
608: 'Awake, awake to love and work!' *Tune: 'Sheltered Dale'*
619: 'We meet you, O Christ' *Tune: 'Paderhorn'*

8. Swiss:

367: 'I want to walk with Jesus Christ' *Tune: 'Helvetia'*
463: 'Now let us from this table rise' *Tune: 'Solothurn'*

9. Swedish:

117: 'O Lord my God, when I in awesome wonder'
  Tune: 'How great thou art'

10. Polish:

149: 'Infant holy' *Tune: 'Infant holy'*

11. Basque:

139: 'The Angel Gabriel from heaven came'
  Tune: 'Gabriel's Message'
146: 'Away in a manger, no crib for a bed'
  Tune: 'Normandy'

12. Finnish:

529: 'Light of the minds that know him' *Tune: 'Nyland'*

13. Dutch:

248: 'This joyful Eastertide' *Tune: 'Vreuchten'*

Tour 7:
Psalms Rediscovered

he Book of Psalms is the hymn book of the Bible. As such you will find the same rich spread of themes that appear in 'Rejoice and Sing' or any full-scale hymn book. There is proclamation: announcing the outpouring of God's activity in mercy and justice, in patience and suffering. Then there is response: in song, we meet the full spread of human emotion and struggle as people like ourselves try and understand God's personality and priorities for the world. Proclamation and response: in the Psalms we have set before us in song first 'God's creating and redeeming love' and then 'Creation's response to God's love', the two main sections in the ordering of 'Rejoice and Sing'.

Christians for centuries saw in the Psalms their main source of poetry and music, expressing their own hopes and fears. They have seen there pictures of God which reminded them of Jesus. Ask many Christians today what their favourite piece of Scripture is and they will respond: 'The Lord is my Shepherd'. They say this because they not only see God's personal protection and guiding in the words of the Psalm. They also recall Jesus the 'Good Shepherd' who came and showed the world what God's love meant and how it could be experienced.

The storehouse is still there. It is still full to overflowing. In 'Rejoice and Sing' it now forms a separate section of the book, and much time and thought has been put into its arrangement and content. The hope was and is that this resource will be used for reading in public worship, for meditation in private devotion, and for singing by choir and congregation in a variety of ways.

The Canticles which complete the main Psalmody section are closely linked in many ways. They are made up of other passages from the Scriptures which are helpful in worship in the same way that the Psalms are. They are printed in a similar style, given similar musical settings and offer the same opportunity for responsive reading, singing and praying.

This tour will encourage you not to neglect this treasure trove.

William White, in his comments on Chanting in 'Rejoice and Sing' (p.959) writes: '...do not let chanting be dull: with fluent articulation there must be a vivid expression of meaning and mood, whether it be tenderness or triumph, prayer or praise. Herein lies our true worship.'

These words could be applied to the Psalms and Canticles in whatever form they are sung or spoken. There is no need for this section of the book to be seen as dead wood from the ancient past. We must expect to be surprised by the passion of the words and the beauty of some of the music. Then we will be in a state of mind and heart to receive what is best from the hymnwriters and poets of the Bible.

This tour will help us discover ways into the Psalms so that they become a cherished friend, an eager resource, a place to return to again and again.

Singing the Psalms

Page 958 of the full edition of 'Rejoice and Sing' introduces the musical settings of the Psalms in the hymnbook. It outlines four types of settings, three in metre and one in prose:

1. METRICAL:

These are more like 'hymns' in that they are set out in lines of 'poetry' (though often it is only the second and fourth lines which rhyme). Many are in Common Metre (CM) but there has been an attempt to provide considerable variation in 'Rejoice and Sing'.
Here is a selection:

669   **PSALM 1:**
'Happy are they who walk in God's wise way'
Tune: 'Sri Lampang'
Notes on this Psalm appear in the Global Tour (No.6).
The compilers are already being adventurous. This
melody from Thailand gives a special flavour to the
words.

671   **PSALM 13:**
'How long, O Lord, will you forget me?'
Tune: 'New Thirteenth'
The opening verses of Psalm 13 are here paraphrased and
set to a minor key tune which gives it the necessary
yearning and pathos. John Bell and Graham Maule of
the Iona community are responsible for the words and
music. It is particularly suitable for Good Friday, and
can be dramatic if sung unaccompanied.

674   **PSALM 19: 'God's perfect law revives the soul'**
Tune: 'Allein Gott'
A Psalm suitable especially for Bible Sunday or for
Ordination and Induction services, it can also be used as
a response by choir or music group when the Scriptures
are read or preaching is about to take place. The second
verse contains the well known verse: 'May the words of
my mouth and the meditation of my heart be acceptable
to you, O Lord, my rock and my redeemer.' (Psalm 19.14)

677   **PSALM 23: 'The God of love my Shepherd is'**
Tune: 'University'
This setting of Psalm 23 has been commented on in the
Historical Tour (No.2) under the name of George Herbert.

679   **PSALM 23:**
'The Lord's my Shepherd, I'll not want'
Tune: 'Crimond'
Perhaps the best known Psalm or hymn in the book.
An alternative tune is suggested in case you don't know
'Crimond'!

681   **PSALM 24:**
'Ye gates, lift up your heads on high'
Tune: 'St George's, Edinburgh'
If you live north of Hadrian's wall, (or a little further
south even) this too will be your national anthem.
Suitable on many occasions, its words are particularly
applicable to Palm Sunday, Easter Day or Ascension.
The Alleluias are magnificent and could be used
independently for Easter Day, as a prayer response or
a call to worship.

684   **PSALM 27: 'God is my strong salvation'**
Tune: 'Christus der ist mein leben'
James Montgomery's version of part of Psalm 27 is one of those which could appear in Tour 11 of this book for its theme is the individual's dependence upon God in time of difficulty.

685   **PSALM 34:**
'Through all the changing scenes of life'
Tune: 'Wiltshire'
This is a well known paraphrase of Psalm 34 but many will have known it in the past as a 'hymn'. Here is a Metrical Psalm which will be used frequently in worship.

689   **PSALM 42:**
'As pants the hart for cooling streams'
Tune: 'Martyrdom'
'As a deer longs for flowing streams, so my soul longs for you, O God'. Psalm 42 is beautiful song from a tormented and lonely individual. The metrical version leaves out a great deal of the pain in the Psalm though there are hints in verse 3. The Psalm ends in strong hope.

691   **PSALM 46:**
'God is our refuge and our strength'
Tune: 'Stroudwater'
A Scottish paraphrase which is much loved and much sung.

695   **PSALM 51:**
'O God be gracious to me in your love'
Tune: Song 24'
After a whole series of Common Metre psalms it is good to come to one with longer lines! Ian Pitt-Watson has done us a great service in tastefully paraphrasing a number of the Psalms.

697   **PSALM 63: 'O God, thou art my God alone'**
Tune: 'Wainwright'
Another James Montgomery piece which has some beautiful lines. A splendid Psalm for congregational singing.

703   **PSALM 84: 'How lovely is thy dwelling-place'**
Tune: 'Harington (Retirement)'
But for Psalm 23 this would be top of the pops for Metrical Psalms. The tune Harington started life off as a 'glee' so there's a surprise for you!

705   **PSALM 90: 'Our God, our help in ages past'**
Tune: 'St Anne'
*Sung on many a Remembrance Sunday, this Psalm merits
an outing on many more occasions in the year. New Year
would be equally suitable. Note the first word is 'Our'
not 'O'! Note also the change in wording in verse 5
('years' replaces 'sons') , an alteration which is actually
more accurate to Psalm 90.9-10, though it will not meet
with universal approval!*

709   **PSALM 98: 'New songs of celebration render'**
Tune: 'Rendez à Dieu'
*Erik Routley's brilliant version of Psalm 98 has been
acclaimed widely as a superb paraphrase. Verse 1 makes
a splendid introit. Verse two adds the whole orchestra.
Verse three adds the whole of the created universe. What
more do you want?*

712   **PSALM 100: 'All people that on earth do dwell'**
Tune: 'Old Hundredth'
*Classic metrical version to an equally classic tune, often
number one in hymn books. It is so familiar we have
ceased to be surprised at the words. They have changed
over the years. For a while 'fear' replaced 'mirth' in verse
one. The punctuation in verse 4 in interesting. After the
word 'why' Congregational Praise had a comma, Church
Hymnary III had a question mark, and now we have a
colon! The sense seems to be: 'Why do we do all this?
Because God is good, his mercy is for ever more.' The colon
or question mark seem best. You choose!*

716   **PSALM 103: 'My soul repeat his praise'**
Tune: 'Dundrennan'
*For notes on this excellent Psalm and tune, see Hidden
Gems Tour (No.5) where 'Dundrennan' comes under the
section on Music Gems.*

720   **PSALM 113: 'Praise the Lord!'**
Tune: 'Laudate Pueri'
*If you were familiar with New Church Praise then you
may have been introduced to this version. It has quite a
rhythm, and could have a clapping accompaniment.*

723   **PSALM 117:**
'From all that dwell below the skies'
Tune: 'Lasst uns erfreuen'
*This is an Isaac Watts' Doxology which makes a
resounding conclusion to any act of worship. Vaughan
Williams' arrangement of this tune is also very popular.
Add a trumpet and it's perfect.*

726   PSALM 121: 'I to the hills will lift mine eyes'
Tune: 'Dundee (French)'
Psalm 121 is one of those Psalms which needs both a
prose and a metrical version in any hymnbook. This is
the metrical version to the well-loved Scottish Psalter
tune 'Dundee (French)'.

731   PSALM 139:
'You are before me, Lord, you are behind'
Tune: 'Sursum Corda'
This excellent paraphrase has been recommended in the
Introductory Tour (No.1)

734   PSALM 146:
'I'll praise my maker while I've breath'
Tune: 'Lucerne (Dresden)'
This is a magnificent version of Psalm 146 and will be
remembered by many as No.8 in Congregational Praise.
To John Wesley it was a special favourite and he was
heard trying to repeat it on his death bed. If you haven't
discovered it yet, then don't wait that long.

740   MAGNIFICAT:
'Tell out, my soul, the greatness of the Lord'
Tune: 'Woodlands'
You may be surprised to find this hymn among the
Canticles rather than in the Advent section of the
hymnbook. It is a paraphrase of the Magnificat and so
has its rightful place here. John Wilson wrote a descant
which unfortunately didn't find its way into this book
but can be found in Hymns and Psalms Methodist and
Ecumenical Hymn Book (No. 86).

750   'All praise to thee, for thou, O King divine'
Tune: 'Fredericktown'
This hymn is probably the best paraphrase of Philippians
2. 5-11. In the cantitcles it is entitled 'A Song of Christ's
Glory'. Although it goes well to 'Sine Nomine' (No. 658)
the compilers have introduced a new tune 'Fredericktown'
which is refreshing and not beyond most congregations.
The Alleluias are incorporated rather than separated and
are unusual in that they have a dotted rhythm.

751   'Come, Holy Ghost, our souls inspire'
Tune: 'Veni Creator Spiritus'
An ancient hymn in its plain-song setting. Some would
feel that this combination of words and music is best
sung in a cold cathedral in the dead of winter with no
heat on. This may be an instance where it would have
been better for the whole hymn to be interlined because it

*is sometimes difficult to fit the words in. The Doxology,
however, is printed that way and it helps.*

755 **'We praise, we worship thee, O God'**
Tune: 'Mainzer'
Here is one of three ways in 'Rejoice and Sing' *to
celebrate the 'Te Deum'. 'Mainzer' is well known so
perhaps this is the easiest of the three options. It is
important that we do sing the 'Te Deum' for it is a
complete act of praise. It can be sung in the communion
service as the act of thanksgiving.*

2. ANGLICAN CHANTING

Anglican Chanting may be out of vogue in the Free
Churches but it is not as difficult or off-putting as
many think. The fact that some of us were brought up
in churches which did it regularly - and with little pain -
is evidence that it can be done. The only difference is
probably the demise of choirs thus removing the lead
they gave to this way of chanting.

The point (sorry! 'aim') of Anglican chanting is to
preserve the speech pattern. The length of notes and the
rhythm are determined by the way you would normally
say the sentence. William White has written a page of
notes on 'how' to do it on page 959 of the Full Edition of
'Rejoice and Sing'.

You must remember that the **bold type** is to enable
the Psalms to be read responsively. It does not have
anything to do with the singing of the chants.

The following Psalms and Canticles have been set for Anglican
Chant:

Psalm 18: (672) 'I love you O Lord my strength'
Psalm 19: (673) 'The heavens declare the glory of God'
Psalm 20: (675) 'May the Lord answer you in the day of trouble'
Psalm 22: (676) 'My God, my God, why have you forsaken me'
Psalm 25: (682) 'To you, O Lord, I lift up my soul'
Psalm 34: (686) 'I will bless the Lord at all times'
Psalm 46: (692) 'God is our refuge and strength'
Psalm 51: (694) 'Have mercy on me, O God, according to your
loving-kindness'
Psalm 62: (696) 'For God alone my soul in silence waits'
Psalm 72: (700) 'Give the king your justice, O God'

Psalm 80: (701) 'Hear, O Shepherd of Israel, leading Joseph like
a flock'
Psalm 91: (706) 'They who dwell in the shadow of the Most High'
Psalm 98: (710) 'Sing to the Lord a new song'
Psalm 103: (714) 'Bless the Lord O my soul'
Psalm 107: (718) 'Give thanks to the Lord for he is good'
Psalm 111: (719) 'Alleluia! I will give thanks to the Lord with my
whole heart'
Psalm 116: (721) 'I love the Lord, because he has heard the voice of
my supplication'
Psalm 118: (724) 'The Lord is my strength and my song'
Psalm 130: (728) 'Out of the depths I have called to you O Lord'
Psalm 139: (730) 'Lord, you have searched me out and known me'
Psalm 145: (733) 'The Lord is gracious and full of compassion'
Venite: (736) 'O come let us sing to the Lord'
Benedictus: (738) 'Blessed be the Lord God of Israel'
Magnificat: (739) 'My soul proclaims the greatness of the Lord'
Nunc Dimittis: (742 First Version)
'Now, Lord, let your servant go in peace'
A Song of Resurrection: (748)
'Christ our Passover has been sacrificed for us'
A Song of Christ's Glory: (749) 'Christ Jesus was in the form of God'
Te Deum: (756) 'We praise you O God, we acclaim you as Lord'

Starting for the first time? Try Psalm 19 (No. 673) or Psalm
46 (No.692). Read each verse out loud first so that you can
hear the normal rhythm of the words. Then listen to the
tune a number of times until it is familiar. Then try fitting
the words into the tune changing note where there is a
vertical line. Take it slowly at first. Try and make it sound
like speech.

3. | PSALM TONES

Another and increasingly popular way to sing the
Psalms and Canticles is using Psalm 'Tones'. On Page
958 of '*Rejoice and Sing*' there are notes on the way
to use these settings. Each line begins with a reciting
note to which one or a number of syllables may be
given. You sing all the words on this note until you
have three syllables left. A line is put in the printed
text where this change occurs. In the musical text the
last three notes are two black (short) notes followed by
a white (long) one.

Each of these settings has an 'Antiphon' or sung response which is optional, but which may be the best starting point when learning to appreciate these Psalms. It is usually sung at the beginning and at the end of the Psalm. A list of all antiphons in *Rejoice and Sing* is found in the 'Short Excursions' tour (No. 10) Section 5.

First let us list the Psalms and Canticles which are sung this way:

Psalm 65:   (698) 'You are to be praised, O God, in Zion'
Psalm 96:   (708) 'Sing to the Lord a new song'
Psalm 100: (711) 'Be joyful in the Lord, all you lands'
Psalm 121: (725) 'I lift my eyes to the hills'
Psalm 131: (729) 'O Lord, I am not proud'
Psalm 145: (733) 'The Lord is gracious and full of compassion'
A Song of the Incarnation: (741)
                 'The grace of God has dawned upon the world'
Nunc Dimittis: (742 Second Version)
                 'Now, Lord, let your servant go in peace'
Salvator Mundi: (747)
                 'Saviour of the world, Lord Jesus, Son of God'
A Song of the First-born: (752)
                 'Christ is the image of the unseen God'

Brenda Stephenson, who has composed a number of the tones and antiphons in *Rejoice and Sing* recommends that the learning of a particular Psalm Tone and Response should be spread out over a number of weeks.

Following her advice I would suggest a possible programme for learning may be as follows:

Week 1:
   Antiphon used for incidental music on organ or piano
   Singing group rehearse antiphon

Week 2:
   Nunc Dimittis read responsively at close of worship.
   Antiphon sung by singing group
   Soloist or singing group rehearse Tone

Week 3:
   Singing group or soloist sing Tone
   Congregation and singing group sing Antiphon

Week 4:
   All sing Tone
   All sing Antiphon

The Second version of the Nunc Dimittis (No. 742) makes a good introduction because the words are relatively familiar and the antiphon is very melodic.

Follow this similarly using Psalm 100, (No. 711) which can be used at the beginning of worship. Remember that antiphons can be used independently as prayer responses within worship.

4. 'GELINEAU' AND 'GREGORY MURRAY' STYLE

The final setting for singing Psalms and Canticles is that using what we call the Grail text and which are sung with 'tones' and 'antiphons' but where the tone changes bar by bar in the music. The text for these Psalms is printed between the staves of music in the Full Edition and below the Melody line in the Melody edition so that you can see clearly where the music changes. This time the word or syllable on which you change tone is printed in bold type, so when these Psalms are used for responsive readings it is best if the leader reads all the verses and the congregation responds with the spoken Antiphon.

The Psalms and canticles which are set in this form are:

Psalm   8: (670)   'How great is your name, O Lord,
                      our God - through all the earth'
Psalm   23: (678)   'The Lord is my Shepherd, there is
                      nothing I shall want'
Psalm   24: (680)   'The Lord's is the earth and its
                      fulness'
Psalm   47: (693)   'All peoples clap your hands'
Psalm   67: (699)   'O God, be gracious and bless us'
Psalm   84: (702)   'How lovely is your dwelling place,
                      O Lord of hosts'
Psalm 150:   (735)   'O praise God in his holiness'
                     (same style but no antiphon)
Beatitudes: (743)   'Blest are the poor in spirit'
A Song of Praise for all the Saints: (754)
                     'Lord, we remember your people'
Te Deum: (757)   'You we praise as God'

Included in this list are three pieces which approximate but are not strictly in this style of singing. They are Psalm 150 (No. 735), the Beatitudes (No. 743), and A Song of Praise for all the Saints (No. 754).

If you are introducing these chants for the first time then the same time and care should be taken as has been suggested in section 3. There are some splendid antiphons among these Psalms and their exploration is thoroughly recommended. The Gelineau setting of Psalm 23 is particularly atmospheric with a contrasting Antiphon which must not be taken too fast. Glide gracefully over the running notes.

POST SCRIPT

Three pieces from this section have not been mentioned because they do not fit into any definable category. They merit brief attention before this tour ends.

713: **'Jubilate, everybody'**
Since this contemporary chorus is based closely upon verses of Psalm 100, it is included in the Psalm section of the hymnbook. If you have been searching frantically for it, here it is!

745: **'A New Commandment I give unto you'**
Here an important text from John's Gospel is set to music. It is particularly useful for communion services and for Maundy Thursday.

746: **'God, your glory we have seen in your Son'**
Brian Wren's translation of these verses has given us a dramatic taste of the French original. Unfortunately the music is not easy! It must be hoped that some adventurous worship groups will have a positive look at this Canticle and see how it can be shared. The words make the strongest possible dismissal from worship. The Words Only tour (No.8) will also be recommending this hymn.

Tour 8: Words Only

When you walk into church on a Sunday and are given a hymnbook and a big smile then you have something to smile about. In your hands you have the beautiful words of writers and poets down the centuries: thousands of words, all of them communicating good news of great joy for all people.

Even if you never sing a note, the words are there. The hearts and lives of the saints present and past are open like a book for you to draw on. Read on, saint, read on.

In public worship this reservoir is always full, always ready for us to drink deeply. What a shame to miss most of it because only five hymns are sung in the worship at the most.

This tour explores ways of using the words of 'Rejoice and Sing' to enrich our worship. The words can be used for all sorts of situations.

We will look at five particular areas:
1. Choral Reading
2. Prayers
3. The Beginning and End of Worship
4. Poems and Meditations
5. Hymns as the basis for Drama, Dance and Visual Display

1. CHORAL READING

There is a great deal of material in 'Rejoice and Sing' which can be used for Choral Reading. It falls into three areas:
1. Liturgical material
2. Psalms and Canticles
3. Hymns

1. Liturgical material

'Rejoice and Sing' prints Prayers and Responses for
Worship at the beginning of the book. This section
comprises numbers 4-20. Leader's words are in
normal type and the responses for congregation are
in **bold type.**

Confessions of faith are at the back of the book:
 759 The Apostles' Creed (not in bold print but clearly
    to be read by all)
 760 The Nicene Creed (not in bold print but clearly
    to be read by all)
 761 The Nature Faith and Order of the United
    Reformed Church (responsive version)

2. Psalms and Canticles

These are set out for responsive reading and this should
be encouraged. Again, the normal print is for the Leader
and the bold print is for the Congregation. The only
exception is the 'Gelineau' and 'Gregory Murray' style
material where bold print is used to indicate the start of
a new tone and a new bar of music, so in these case the
Leader should read all the verses of the Psalm and the
Congregation respond with the words of the Antiphon.
For a list of these Psalms please see the previous tour
(No.8.) section 4.

One Metrical Psalm paraphrase which lends itself to
good choral reading is Psalm 113, (No. 720): 'Praise the
Lord! Praise, you servants of the Lord'.

The verses may be split up as follows:
All: Praise the Lord!
Leader: Praise, you servants of the Lord,
        praise the name of the Lord!
Men (or left)   Blessed be the name of the Lord!
Women (or right) Blessed be the name of the Lord
All: from this time forth and for evermore!
Leader: Praise the Lord!
All: Praise the Lord!

3. Hymns

A number of hymns provide texts which can be read
chorally. The following are a selection:

36: **'St Patrick's breastplate'**
*Verses 1-4 can be split between male and female
(or right and left) parts, followed by verse 5 sung and
verse 6 sung. Verse 5 can be split up for male and
female singing very effectively, or choir/congregation.*

45: **'Morning has broken'**
*The contrast between the first four lines and second four
lines of each verse can be brought out in singing or choral
reading by using different groups of voices.*

107: **'The love of God comes close'**
*This hymn has a good shape for choral reading: lines 1-4
of each verse for one set of voices followed by lines 5-7
for a second set. Short prayers of intercession may also
be interspersed.*

114: **'Let all the world in every corner sing'**
*Because of the way this famous hymn is set out, it is
easy to see how it could be 'proclaimed' by leader and
congregation.*

142: **'Now tell us, gentle Mary'**
*Not so much a choral reading as a dialogue between two
people. It divides naturally half way through each verse.*

152: **'Ring a bell for peace'**
*Voice 1, lines 1 and 2; All, line 3; Voice 2, lines 4 and 5;
All, line 6. Instruments can be added between the verses.*

165: **'The poor and the humble'**
*The chorus can be spoken by congregation in response to
voices reading the verses.*

207: **'My song is love unknown'**
*Familiar words such as these can receive new vitality
through choral reading. They can be split in many ways.
Try: Verse 1, single voice; verse 2, all (lines 1-4) followed
by single voice (lines 5-8); verse 3: all (loud); verse 4,
women (soft); verse 5, men; verse 6, single voice; verse 7,
single voice (lines 1-4), all (lines 5-8).*

265: **'I cannot tell why he, whom angels worship'**
*Two voices or sets of voices can read these long verses,
splitting each one after line 4.*

292: **'When morning gilds the skies'**
Clearly, this is good choral material. Divide voices plus chorus as you wish.

329: **'There's a spirit in the air'**
Again there are many options open with these words.

422: **'Lift high the Cross, the love of Christ proclaim'**
Different readers can be asked to read the verses with the congregation joining in the refrain, sung or spoken.

473: **'God is love, and where true love is, God himself is there'**
The first two verses and refrain form an excellent call to worship.

478: **'Many are the lightbeams'**
These lines can be read alternatively by leader and congregation.

607: **'This is the truth we hold'**
A marvellous proclamatory hymn like this makes a strong choral reading. The two phrases 'Christ has died' and 'Christ is risen' could be given to two sides of the congregation with the final line spoken together. Individual voices may do the opening four lines of each verse.

639: **'This we can do for justice and for peace'**
Another splendid hymn for announcing together! Each verse may be divided into voices as follows:

Part A: This we can do for justice and for peace:
Part B: we can pray, and work to answer prayers that other people say.
Part A: This we can do in faith and see it through –
All: for Jesus is alive today.

641: **'We pray for peace'**
For choral reading take verses 1-4 only and give lines 1,5,6 to one voice or set of voices. Then give lines 2,3,4 to another voice or voices. Verse 5 may be read by all. Then verse 6 may be read by an individual as a prayer or it may revert to the pattern of verses 1-4.

2. PRAYERS

There are many hymns which, when read aloud by an individual, form excellent prayers for public worship. Here is a list of some of the hymns which can be used in this way. Some have lines which make suitable congregational responses:

The prayers inside the back and front covers of the hymnbook

26: 'Father, we praise you, now the night is over'
(response: line 4)
42: 'For the fruits of all creation' *(response: lines 2,4,8)*
66: 'My God, I thank thee, who hast made'
(can be 'we' instead of 'I')
87: 'Lord, bring the day to pass'
(response: lines 5,6; vs 4: line 6 only)
110: 'Father, we thank you' *(thanksgiving)*
126: 'O come, O come, Immanuel' *(response: lines 5,6)*
138: 'Come, thou long-expected Jesus' *(Advent)*
145: 'O Holy Child of Bethlehem' *(verse 4 only)*
146: 'Be near me, Lord Jesus, I ask you to stay' *(verse 2 only)*
270: 'Lord, Christ, when first you came to earth' *(confession)*
302: 'O Breath of life, come sweeping through us' *(Pentecost)*
338: 'Stay with us, God, as longed-for peace eludes us'
(petition)
404: 'Lord of all good, our gifts we bring to thee' *(offertory)*
444: 'Father, we give you thanks, who planted'
(thanksgiving and petition)
465: 'With grateful hearts our faith professing' *(Baptism)*
493: 'Dear Master, in whose life I see' *(confession)*
495: 'Father, hear the prayer we offer' *(petition)*
497: 'Give to me, Lord, a thankful heart' *(petition)*
498: 'God be in my head' *(petition)*
506: 'Jesus, thy boundless love to me' *(petition)*
508: 'O Jesus Christ, grow thou in me' *(petition)*
510: 'O Lord, you are the light of the world' *(petition)*
516: 'We praise you , Lord, for all that's true and pure'
(thanksgiving)
528: 'Jesus, good above all other' *(response: line 4)*
568: 'Lord Christ, the Father's mighty Son' *(Christian Unity)*
618: 'We give thee but thine own' *(offertory)*
621: 'Almighty Father, who for us thy Son didst give'
(petition)
646: 'Help us accept each other' *(petition)*
651: 'O God, by whose almighty plan' *(response: lines 5,6)*

THE BEGINNING AND END OF WORSHIP

The hymnbook is a fine resource for providing imaginative material to commence worship or to send people out with joy and confidence. The Psalms have often been used in this way and they should be familiar to worship leaders. What are less familiar are hymns which are also suitable.

Some of these are as follows:

The prayers inside the front cover of the hymnbook
Numbers 1, 2, 18 and 19 from the opening Order of Worship.

45:   'Morning has broken'
       (choral reading as recommended in section 1)
60:   'God who spoke in the beginning' (call to worship)
111: 'In praise of God meet duty and delight'
       (call to worship, select verses)
172: 'From east to west, from shore to shore'
       (Christmas call to worship: selected verses)
260: 'Christ is alive! Let Christians sing'
       (Easter call to worship: selected verses)
272: 'Glory to God the Father' (dismissal: verse 4)
292: 'When morning gilds the skies'
       (choral reading as recommended in section 1)
306: 'Spirit of flame, whose living glow'
       (Pentecost call to worship: especially verses 1,2)
339: 'Great God, your love has called us here'
       (call to worship: verses 1,2,5)
414: 'When, in our music, God is glorified'
       (call to worship: selected verses)
426: 'We know that Christ is raised and dies no more'
       (Easter call to worship: verses 1,3,4)
435: 'Christian people, raise your song'
       (Easter/Communion call to worship)
438: 'No end there is! We depart in peace'
       (Verse 4: Communion dismissal)
447: 'Together met, together bound'
       (Verse 5, Communion dismissal)
453: 'Jesus call us in, sends us out'
       (Verse 3: Communion dismissal)
468: 'Surprised by joy no song can tell'
       (Wedding: call to worship)
473: 'God is love, and where true love is...'
       (choral reading as recommended in section 1)
480: 'The church is like a table'
       (call to worship: selected verses)

569: 'We pause to give thanks'
    (call to worship, verse 1; dismissal, verse 3)
574: 'Go forth and tell! The doors are open wide'
    (Verses 3 and 4: dismissal)
602: 'Forth in the peace of Christ, we go'
    (dismissal, suggest verses 2,3,4,1)
746: 'God, your glory we have seen in your Son'
    (verse 5: dismissal)

4. POEMS AND MEDITATIONS

Worship can be enriched by the wise use of poetry and meditations, chosen to shed light on the particular theme of the occasion. The hymnbook contains much to help the leader(s) of worship discover such material. Careful thought needs to be given as to how such texts can be best used. Words are precious. They cannot be rushed over or gabbled. With good preparation, however, the texts of some hymns can be communicated in a powerful and sensitive way which cannot easily be achieved when the words are sung by congregations.

In some instances music can be used effectively in the background of readings. It must not distract, but simply add colour. With selected hymns it is possible to read the hymn to the rhythm of the hymn tune (eg. No. 44). With practice this can be most dramatic. Sometimes music can be played between verses to provide space and time for words to be absorbed and reflected upon.

Some of the more suitable hymns for reading in this way are as follows:

44: 'Lord of the boundless curves of space'
    (try reading to the tune 'San Rocco')
64: 'I lift my eyes to the quiet hills'
    (try reading to the tune 'Davos')
80: 'Can we by searching find out God'
85: 'God in his love for us lent us this planet'
99: 'Morning glory, starlit sky' *(try reading to tune 'Emma')*
136: 'And art thou come with us to dwell' *(Advent)*
154: 'From heaven above to earth I come' *(Christmas)*
162: 'In the bleak mid-winter' *(Christmas or Epiphany)*
170: 'What child is this, who, laid to rest' *(Christmas)*
174: 'Where is this stupendous stranger?'
    (Christmas or Epiphany)
175: 'Lo, how a rose is growing'
    (Christmas, add music to reading)

178: 'Who would think that what was needed'
   (Christmas or Epiphany)
180: 'Before the world began' *(Christmas or Epiphany)*
186: 'Lord, when the wise men came from far' *(Epiphany)*
198: 'A stranger once did bless the earth'
214: 'Before the cock crew twice' *(Holy Week)*
215: 'Ah, holy Jesus, how hast thou offended'
   (play set tune between selected verses)
219: 'Nature with open volume stands' *(Good Friday)*
221: 'To mock your reign, O dearest Lord' *(Good Friday)*
225: 'Here hangs a man discarded' *(Good Friday)*
243: 'Now the green blade rises from the buried grain'
   (Easter)
307: 'Though gifts of knowledge and of tongues'
   (1 Corinthians 13)
339: 'Great God, your love has called us here'
340: 'I have no bucket, and the well is deep'
352: 'Come my Way, my Truth, my Life'
354: 'Come, living God, when least expected'
362: 'Lord Jesus, in the days of old' *(Emmaus)*
466: 'As man and woman we were made' *(wedding)*
482: 'We are not our own. Earth forms us'
525: 'He comes to us as one unknown' *(Emmaus)*
548: 'Nothing distress you, nothing affright you.'
609: 'Am I my brother's keeper?'

5. HYMNS AS THE BASIS FOR DRAMA, DANCE AND VISUAL DISPLAY

All that we have said so far has been to enhance the
availability and use of the words of hymns in *'Rejoice
and Sing'*. There is one enormous danger in all this:
we can give the impression that words are the be-all
and end-all of everything. They may be one of our main
ways of communicating but they are not alone. Words
need space. They need silence. The sound of the human
voice can be oppressive unless it is placed alongside all
the senses which make up the human response.

Worship needs words and music. It needs silence and
reflection. It needs a beautiful setting. It needs colour
and light. It needs physical movement.

How can the words of hymns be used to bring about a
total response from people, so that their lives are filled
with awe and wonder, with new insight and hope?

Many of the poems in section 4 of this tour can be shared through movement, mime, dance, and colourful posters and banners. The same could be said of some of the 'Personal' material which will be highlighted in the final tour (No.11).

Christian Education groups can use hymns as the basis for their discovery of major Christian themes or festivals, and the words can be displayed in countless ways through calligraphy, collage, and needlework.

Hymn texts old and new form ideal material on which to base the themes for flower or handicraft festivals.

Only a few examples of suitable hymns can be given here, for much depends upon the imagination and initiative in each local setting. Suffice it to say, leave no imaginative stone unturned to communicate the Gospel through the words of hymns.

Here are a few hymns to set you exploring:

52: **'To God who makes all lovely things'**
This hymn is full of pictures and can form the basis for a visual display suitable for Harvest or Autumn.

175: **'Lo, how a rose is growing'**
There must be a way of using lights and flowers to portray the message of this hymn, possible in a Christmas evening festival.

195: **'I danced in the morning'**
When this hymn is sung it seems to be over before you have taken a breath. The words are powerful and will lend themselves to dance and mime. Music could be played between verses to give the words some space. Visual images abound so there is plenty of opportunity to make these words live.

199: **'Jesus the Lord says, I am the bread'**
The symbols from John's Gospel which form the basis of this hymn can be brought up and displayed while the hymn is sung. New verses can be written without difficulty if you wish to add to the number.

207: **'My song is love unknown'**
This hymn has already been suggested for choral reading. It is a narrative hymn and paints a series of different scenes in Jesus life and ministry: plenty of material for drama, mime, or display.

249: **'Too early for the blackbird'**
Another hymn which tells a story and therefore is suitable for simple mime or to expand with Scripture readings to shed light on the narrative. So once you have learnt the tune and the words, that is only the beginning of what can be achieved.

325: **'Into a world of dark'**
This hymn seems to lend itself to a 'Sound and Light' portrayal. In addition liturgical dance can communicate feelings first of darkness and disorder and then of emerging light and possibility.

334: **'Walking in a garden'**
Three garden scenes are portrayed in these verses, giving the opportunity to create three scenes from which the theme can be explored. The hymn text can be spread throughout an act of worship with readings to provide a 'garden' theme.

517: **'As the bride is to her chosen'**
More pictures, images, all sitting up waiting to be portrayed through a variety of media.

474: **'Brother, sister, let me serve you'**
Since this hymn speaks to intensely personal situations it is an ideal one for simple dance or mime.

Psalms and Canticles: Many of the Psalms can be mimed or danced. Some speak of personal tragedy and pain, some of deep questioning and searching, some of thanksgiving and delight. An individual dancer can help a congregation experience the depths and heights of these songs. Psalm 139 (No.730) is a good example and may be a good starting point for this exploration. A very short piece like 'A New Commandment' (No.745) can also lend itself to simple mime.

Tour 9: A Capella

I t is sad that singing unaccompanied is often regarded as second-best. In many churches the frantic search for an organist or pianist is evidence of this. And yet, if you go on holiday to the far North West of Scotland you will soon have the opposite impression: organs are anathema. So is music of any kind on Sunday! And if you go to Greece or to Russia you will also discover that unaccompanied singing is the norm. And what singing! The Orthodox churches achieve an incredible quality of sound without accompaniment.

The irony is that the author of this book delights in the sound of a good pipe organ! Nevertheless, the message has come over to him loud and clear: just because we have no organist does not mean we can't sing! It may be that the future of music in our churches lies in improving the quality of our singing. That will first mean we should hear each other sing. And that can only be achieved without an organ! That is why when you come to learn a new tune the best way of learning is by hearing a voice sing it to you.

All this is leading to a brief tour which is called 'A Capella'. Which hymns in '*Rejoice and Sing*' are most suitable for unaccompanied singing? If we have no instrument except the voices God has given us, where should we begin?

For a start there is material which can only be sung unaccompanied

For instance there are 'Rounds' and 'Canons'. We can list these so that you can turn to them easily:

ROUNDS AND CANONS

7:	'Gloria'	*(three part canon)*
8:	'Gloria'	*(cantor and response)*
29:	'Father, we adore you'	*(three part round)*
281:	'King of kings and Lord of lords,'	*(two part round)*
286:	'Rejoice in the Lord always'	*(two part round)*
416:	'Glory to thee, my God, this night'	*(two part canon)*
423:	'Wake up, sleeper!'	*(four part round)*
479:	'Shalom Chaverim'	*(four or eight part round)*
512:	'Seek ye first the kingdom of God'	*(two part canon)*

Pentatonic tunes will also fit as canons. Here are three:

92:	'Amazing grace (how sweet the sound)'
181:	'Of the Father's love begotten'
185:	'Wise men seeking Jesus'

Another group of hymns which are particularly suitable for unaccompanied singing are those which are based upon folk songs, or which, written more recently are based on the style of folk singing. Many of these are written for unison singing.

Here are a few which seem to fit the bill:
(omitting familiar Christmas carols!)

FOLK SONGS

45:	'Morning has broken'
48:	'Praise and thanksgiving'
91:	'The right hand of God is writing in our land'
92:	'Amazing grace, (how sweet the sound)'
108:	'The love of God is broad like beach and meadow'
123:	'Think of a world without any flowers'
141:	'Make way, make way, for Christ the King'
164:	'Go, tell it on the mountain'
178:	'Who would think that what was needed'
195:	'I danced in the morning when the world was begun'
197:	'Jesus' hands were kind hands'
199:	'Jesus, the Lord says, I am the bread'
227:	'Were you there when they crucified my Lord?'
234:	'Alleluia, alleluia, give thanks to the risen Lord'
265:	'I cannot tell why he, whom angels worship'
274:	'God is love, his the care'
279:	'I will sing, I will sing a song unto the Lord'
327:	'O God, your love's undying flame'

415: 'You shall go out with joy and be led forth in peace'
438: 'An upper room did our Lord prepare'
452: 'Let us break bread together in the Lord'
453: 'Let us talents and tongues employ'
466: 'As man and woman we were made'
523: 'Give me joy in my heart, keep me praising'
549: 'One more step along the world I go'
555: 'We are marching in the light of God'
558; 'Will you come and follow me'
572: 'Colours of day dawn into the mind'
576: 'God's spirit is deep in my heart'
622: 'Beneath the shade of our vine and fig-tree'
633: 'O let us spread the pollen of peace throughout
        the land'
637: 'The Day of the Lord shall come, as prophets
        have told'
643: 'When Israel was in Egypt's land'
648: 'Jesu, Jesu, fill us with your love'
649: 'Let the world rejoice together, alleluia'
713: 'Jubilate, everybody'

When we come to look at traditional hymns which are
usually written in harmony and ask the question:
'Which are most suitable for unaccompanied singing?',
we have a more difficult task. Clearly, tunes which are
familiar to the congregation will usually go just as well
without accompaniment. Exponents of 'A Capella'
singing will tell you, however, that the best hymns for
singing unaccompanied are those which start either
with a unison line or with a few notes of unison singing,
so that there is a definitive start to each verse. There are
a number of hymns in the hymnbook which fit into this
category. One or two are set in unison throughout but
could still be sung in harmony in parts.

Here are a few:

HYMNS WITH UNISON BEGINNINGS

39:     'All creatures of our God and King'
66:     'My God, I thank thee, who hast made'
79:     'This day God gives me'
104:    'Praise, my soul, the King of heaven'
124:    'We plough the fields, and scatter'
126:    'O come, O come, Immanuel'
199:    'Jesus the Lord says, I am the bread'

237: 'God came in Jesus'
239: 'Jesus lives! Thy terrors now' *(second tune)*
265: 'I cannot tell, why he, whom angels worship'
271: 'You are the King of Glory'
369: 'No more, my God, I boast no more'
457: 'Now, my tongue, the mystery telling'
485: 'Almighty Father, of all things that be'
540: 'Jesus, my Lord, grant your pure grace'
542: 'How good is the God we adore'
599: 'Christ for the world! we sing'
740: 'Tell out, my soul, the greatness of the Lord'

From this brief foray into unaccompanied singing,
there should be enough evidence for you to glimpse
the possibilities. It should not be a last resort! An
unaccompanied verse in the routine singing is a good
idea for it allows the people to hear their own voices and
their neighbours' voices. And if you do find yourselves
in the position of having no 'instrument' apart from
voices, then do all you can to find just one person in the
church or surrounding community who enjoys singing
and has the courage to lead.

Tour 10:
Short Excursions

ome of the most memorable and delightful experiences are short-lived. They are beautiful but they are soon past. But we wouldn't be without them. A 'Short Break' can be refreshing and fulfilling.

'*Rejoice and Sing*' is not filled with five verse hymns and fifty verse Psalms. There are a number of much shorter items which can bring delight to our worship. This tour looks at these in more detail and encourages us to make use of them.

They fall into a number of categories:
1. Prayers and Prayer Responses
2. One verse hymns
3. Liturgical pieces (Glorias, Alleluias, Amens)
4. Doxologies
5. Antiphons
6. Rounds and Canons

Antiphons have received some attention in Tour 7: Sections 3 & 4 of 'Psalms Rediscovered'. A full list is needed and will be included here. Please refer back to the previous tour ('A Capella': Tour 9) for details of Rounds and Canons.

Worship needs short pieces as well as five verse hymns. But they need careful handling. To try and transfer Taizé or Iona to your own back yard is not possible. That's why a service planned solely with Taizé music, for instance, can be a disappointment.

Remember to:

1. Give them space. Don't crowd them with words and activities either side.

2. Give them practice. Don't leave them until last minute. They need as much fore-thought and preparation as longer items in worship.
3. Make sure the congregation know when responses are going to come and how the music will be introduced. In repeated responses there needs to be a minimum of 'playthrough'. A rising arpeggio of three notes is one good way. An improvised entry is fine as long as it is consistent.
4. Give people time to find the place in their hymnbooks
5. Make it clear that they should sit for responses like this.

We will now look at some of the material available in the above categories 1 - 5 and comment on the ways they can be used in worship. When you come to the lists, you will see that the refrains of hymns are also a good source of responsive prayers.

1. PRAYERS AND PRAYER RESPONSES

The words of these responses can be matched to differing themes and seasons. Responses can be built into prayers of confession, thanksgiving, and intercession. They can be used before and after Scripture readings. They can provide items for Introits or Dismissals or for the Offertory Prayer. In Communion services there are responses suitable for sharing while the bread and wine is passed. In devotional services and healing services there is meditative and reflective material.

Here is a selection from which you can choose material for your particular needs and circumstances:

17: 'Lord, I am not worthy to receive you'
36: 'Christ be with me, Christ within me'
      (verse 5 only)
41: 'Gracious God, to thee we raise...' *(refrain only)*
96: 'Great is thy faithfulness' *(refrain only)*

108: 'The love of God is broad like beach and meadow' *(refrain only)*
124: 'All good gifts around us are sent from heaven above' *(refrain only)*
126: 'Rejoice! Rejoice! Immanuel shall come to thee, O Israel' *(refrain only)*
247: 'Thine be the glory, risen, conquering Son' *(refrain only)*
'Yours is the glory, resurrected one' *(refrain only)*
249: 'Chase, chase your gloom and grief away' *(refrain only)*
253: 'Join all on earth, rejoice and sing' *(refrain only)*
268: 'Jesus is Lord, Jesus is Lord!' *(refrain only)*
288: 'Worthy, O Lamb of God, art thou' *(refrain only)*
347: 'Be still and know that I am God'
375: 'In my life, Lord, be glorified, be glorified'
392: 'Holy God, holy and mighty'
393: 'Kindle a flame to lighten the dark'
394: 'Lord, to whom shall we go?'
395: 'No one has ever seen God'
396: 'Lord, we adore you'
397: 'Nothing in all creation'
398: 'O Lord, hear our prayer'
399: 'Stay with us, O Lord Jesus Christ'
400: 'We do not know how to pray as we ought'
401: 'Through our lives and by our prayers'
402: 'Ubi Caritas et amor'
403: 'Laudate, omnes gentes'
452: 'When I fall on my knees...' *(refrain only)*
491: 'Day by day, dear Lord, of thee three things I pray'
627: 'Lead me from death to life, from falsehood to truth'
648: 'Jesu, Jesu, fill us with your love' *(refrain only)*
753: 'Ubi caritas et amor'

2. ONE VERSE HYMNS

Although this list will be short, each piece is a valuable item. One is for the Easter season, one for Baptisms and one for the close of worship.

231: 'Your body in the tomb, your soul in hell'
420: 'The Lord bless you and keep you'
491: 'God be in my head'

In addition it is possible to draw on single verses of hymns as responses within worship. One which comes to mind is hymn No. 332, verse 4: 'Plenteous grace with thee is found' which makes a splendid response following a prayer of Confession.

3. LITURGICAL PIECES

One of the benefits of a good choir is that they can give a strong lead in providing responses for liturgical responses. Congregations can be notoriously sluggish, even to provide a positive 'Amen'! We need to spend more time exploring the range of material given in this section.

The opening items in the Hymnbook concentrate on spoken and sung items for regular use in worship. The list drawn up below also includes refrains from familiar hymns. These are easier to slot into parts of worship because they are already well known.

5a,b,c:	Kyries
6:	Gloria in Excelsis
7:	Gloria *(shortened)*
8:	Gloria *(shortened)*
9a,b,c:	Alleluias
13:	Sanctus
14:	Agnus Dei I
15:	Agnus Dei II
16:	Behold the Lamb of God
20a,b,c,d,e,f:	Amens
163:	Gloria *(refrain only)*
234:	Alleluia, alleluia *(refrain only)*
238:	Alleluia! *(threefold)*
279:	'Allelu, alleluia, glory to the Lord' *(refrain only)*
426:	Alleluia *(threefold, refrain only)*
437:	'Bring bread, bring wine, give glory to the Lord' *(refrain only)*
571:	Alleluia! *(threefold, refrain only)*
665:	'Lord, thy glory fills the heavens' *(refrain only)*
681:	Alleluias and Amens.
693:	'Alleluia, alleluia, alleluia' *(antiphon)*
750:	'Alleluia! Alleluia! Alleluia!' *(refrain only)*

4. DOXOLOGIES

You may be surprised at how many 'Doxologies' there are hidden away in 'Rejoice and Sing'. Again, some of the items are familiar because they come from well loved hymns. As well as making use of Doxologies for the close of worship why not try putting one in when the offertory is brought forward, or after the prayer of dedication. A Doxology is also fitting after the Assurance of Pardon in the early part of the service.

21: 'Praise God, from whom all blessings flow'
22: 'Laud and honour to the Father'
23: 'Unto God be praise and honour'
24: 'Through north and south and east and west'
25: 'To Father, Son and Spirit blest'
72: 'All praise and thanks to God' *(verse 3 only)*
416: 'Praise God from whom all blessing flow' *(verse 6)*
457: 'Praise for ever, thanks and blessing' *(verse 6 only)*
542: 'How good is the God we adore'
600: 'Give God the glory, God and none other'
    (verse 4 only)
659: 'Give God the glory and glad adoration'
    (verse 7 only)
735: 'Glory be to the Father and to the Son...'*(last verse)*
751: 'Praise to thy eternal merit, Father, Son and
    Holy Spirit'
755: 'Glory to thee, O God most high!'
Inside back cover: Gloria Patri *(for chanting)*

5. ANTIPHONS

Most people will be on new territory here. On the 'Psalms Rediscovered' tour you were encouraged to use the Psalms more and more in worship. The Antiphons listed above can be used either with the settings for their own particular Psalm or may be sung quite independently as a response to prayers or to other items in worship. Don't ignore this valuable resource.

114: 'Let all the world in every corner sing
    "My God and King!" ' *(second tune)*
473: 'God is love, and where true love is,
    God himself is there'
670: 'How great is your name, O Lord our God,
    through all the earth'

678: 'The Lord is my Shepherd, nothing shall I want'
680: 'Seek the face of the Lord, and yearn for him'
'Open wide, O you gates eternal, and let the King of glory enter'
693: 'Alleluia, alleluia, alleluia'
698: 'You are to be praised, O God of our salvation'
699: 'Let the peoples praise you, O God,
- let all the peoples praise you!'
702: 'Lord God of hosts, happy are they who trust in you'
708: 'Declare his glory among the nations and his wonders among all peoples'
711: 'Give thanks to the Lord and call upon his name'
725: 'My help comes from the Lord, the maker of heaven and earth'
729: 'Be still, my soul; wait upon the Lord'
733: 'The Lord is near to those who call upon him'
742: 'Save us, Lord, while we are awake, protect us while we sleep'
743: 'Show us your ways, O Lord: teach us your paths'
754: 'Thanks be to God for his saints; they call us to follow Christ our Lord'
757: 'Extol the Lord your God, for the Lord your God is holy'
'Who is the king of glory? The Lord of hosts, he is the king of glory'

Short excursions are essential to our health! Make the most of these items. They present to us an opportunity to involve the congregation more completely in the act of worship. They provide words and music to help us pray, to stimulate silence, and they are one of the best ways of creating an environment in which God's voice can be heard.

Tour 11: Personal

Everyone wants to take their holiday home with them. A stick of Blackpool rock, a bottle of water from the Sea of Galilee, a pound of kippers from the Isle of Man. Then there are the pictures! Yes, the photographs, slides, video: an undeniable record of distant places and broiled flesh, all to bore our friends and neighbours.

What would it be like if we wanted to take souvenirs home from Church? Our concern here is with the hymnbook. Why is it imprisoned in the cupboard from one Sunday to another? Imagine you are a church hymnbook. How do you feel? There's no heat on. You are freezing. It might even be damp. Not very nice is it?

Hymn books are to be used, and there is no better sign of this than to encourage people to take them home and use them to read and explore. They have sung hymns in church. Do the words match up to what happens to people for the rest of the week? Are the composers and authors thinking only of Sunday worshippers? Or are they touching people's lives when they are lonely, and when they are celebrating, when they are grieving and when they are greedy, when they are close to others and when they are distanced through tragedy or failure?

The answer is: take one home and see. This tour will help. Although much of the contents of hymns are related to the community of faith and to the community at large, there are also intensely personal poems and prayers: items which are not meant for public consumption. They may help people in times of pain and distress, in times of need and uncertainty. They may comfort and stir, encourage and challenge. They may remind each of us that the good news of great joy was meant for us individually, for God loves us that way.

The 'Words Only' Tour (No. 8) contains lists of hymns which can be drawn on helpfully for personal devotional use. Section 2 ('Prayers') and Section 4 ('Poems and Meditations') are particularly appropriate.

The sections of 'Rejoice and Sing' which contain most of the personal materials are as follows:

The Need for God:	Hymns 331 - 346
Hearing and Responding	Hymns 347 - 375
Growing in Faith:	Hymns 485 - 516
Discipleship:	Hymns 517 - 538
Pilgrimage:	Hymns 539 - 558

We can now look in more detail at some of the appropriate hymns from these sections and others:

84:   **'Forgive our sins as we forgive'**
Everybody wrestles with the difficulty of forgiveness. Giving and receiving forgiveness can be immensely painful. This hymn reflects upon the problem gracefully and helps us pray about it.

97:   **'King of glory, King of peace'**
George Herbert's beautiful poem has been referred to several times in this book. It speaks to every person, bringing from us gratitude and warmth. The hymn offers back to God the best that we can offer, though this is but minute compared with what is owed to God for his love.

99:   **'Morning glory, starlit sky'**
Again, this hymn has been mentioned a number of times. It is a commentary on the meaning of sacrificial love and is most helpful in our relationships.

218:   **'When my love to God grows weak'**
When we sit and think about what happened to Jesus in the last few days of his life: the loneliness, the disillusionment, the pain, it puts into perspective our own troubles and failures. We need to remember, as this hymn does.

222:   **'My dearest Lord, thy sacred head'**
And so does this one. This hymn has the most intimate language of any hymn as the events of Good Friday come home to...me.

282: **'Most gentle, heavenly Lamb'**
A hymn from Wales which praises Christ in beautiful words for what has been done for our salvation.

300: **'Eternal Spirit of the living Christ'**
Prayer is a mystery and often a struggle to understand and to share. Here is a prayer about prayer, a song to help us let go and allow Christ to be our prayer in time of need.

305: **'Spirit of God, descend upon my heart'**
Enter the private world of a person searching for God's presence. Enter the writer's agony and struggle. And there find comfort because we have all been there. Then there comes the unforgettable line: 'teach me the patience of unanswered prayer'.

326: **'Loving Spirit, loving Spirit'**
The Holy Spirit is all-embracing, reminding us of God's total character, beyond gender yet embracing all genders, beyond race yet embracing all races. These words celebrate that inclusiveness and that availability.

332: **'Jesus, lover of my soul'**
Charles Wesley could speak to the needs of people in all generations because he had a magnificent grasp upon God's grace. These words may be familiar but they merit careful meditation. There are lines here to help many a person in pain, in loss or in guilt, giving a glimpse of light and hope.

340: **'I have no bucket and the well is deep'**
Mentioned in the 'Hidden Gems' tour (No. 5), this is a meditation on the encounter between the woman of Samaria and Jesus. It unlocks the human longing for full life and the possibility that Jesus is the key.

364: **'Just as I am, without one plea'**
When read over and over again, familiar words can reveal new treasures. We need reminding that God welcomes us 'just as we are', though we are 'tossed about with many a conflict, many a doubt'.

365: **'Rock of ages, cleft for me'**
You may not have seen the title for this 'golden oldie'. It is 'A Living and Dying Prayer for the Holiest Believer in the World'. The point behind the title is that even the holiest of saints has committed so much sin that they are hopelessly in debt to God. Augustus Toplady was

convinced that Christ's death cancelled even this massive
debt, so our only hope is to cling to the 'Rock'. What a
hymn about grace!

368: **'I sought the Lord, and afterward I knew'**
This is a beautiful hymn in the most intimate of
language. It expresses the Christian's belief that God's
search for us comes long before our search for God. The
image of Jesus reaching out towards us, enabling us to
walk, is particularly moving.

413: **'What a friend we have in Jesus'**
A hymn whose text and tune have come from the era
of Moody and Sankey yet which has lived on into new
generations. It speaks to personal need in any age.
Behind it are Scripture texts such as Psalm 55.22:
'Cast thy burden upon the Lord, and he shall sustain
thee'.

475: **'God, you meet us in our weakness'**
A remarkably simple hymn which will speak directly and
deeply to people in grief or illness. Its theme is that we
are not alone: God comes to us through his Spirit, and
the visible expression of this is the Church community
and all neighbours who speak and show encouragement
and comfort.

493: **'Dear Master, in whose life I see'**
It is amazing how many people say they have been helped
by this hymn. It seems to strike right at the feelings of
failure which we all carry, knowing that we never live up
to our best aspirations and hopes.

501: **'I greet thee, who my sure Redeemer art'**
The Historical Tour (No.2) highlighted this hymn written
by John Calvin. Verse 1 is in the first person, and reads
like a private prayer. From verse two we move into the
plural, yet the hymn does not lose its intimacy.

505: **'Make me a captive, Lord'**
George Matheson wrote two very popular hymns, this
being one (see also below No. 511). Both are intensely
personal. This hymn reflects on the Pauline paradox of
Christian service: it is both slavery and freedom.

506: **'Jesus, thy boundless love to me'**
Paul Gerhardt's beautiful prayer hymn can be a most
helpful resource for meditation and reflection.

511: **'O Love that wilt not let me go'**
This hymn was written by George Matheson when he was suffering great personal anguish. He said that he wrote it 'with extreme rapidity'. Out of the pain has come words of great beauty and help for people ever since.

513: **'Twixt gleams of joy and clouds of doubt'**
A reflective meditation on God's unchanging dependable grace, which is contrasted with the ups and downs of human life. Amid our changes of mood and circumstance God holds us fast.

534: **'Lord, as I wake I turn to you'**
Here is a prayer for the beginning of the day. Verse 2 may raise a few questions but the hymn has a spirit of thankfulness and directness which should speak to many people.

540: **'O Jesu mawr, rho d'anian bur'**
'Jesus, my Lord, grant your pure grace'
A most humble and moving hymn which speaks for itself. It seems in some lines to allude to the experience of Mary Magdalene.

590: **'In heavenly love abiding'**
Anna Waring's hymn is known and loved right across the Christian church. Verse 1 draws on storm imagery and also has an interesting use of the word 'without' (line 5) where it means 'outside' as in the Scottish 'outwith'. Another memorable example of this comes in the original words for 'There is a green hill far away 'without' a city wall'. Verses 2 & 3 use imaginatively the words and pictures in Psalm 23.

591: **'Do not be afraid, for I have redeemed you'**
The opening verses of Isaiah 43 form the backdrop for this hymn. Remember that the original reading is both individual and corporate. The hymn does try and bring out both elements in this.

593: **'O Lord, I would delight in thee'**
God's abundance, never drained, is the theme of this fine hymn.

640: **'Saviour, again, to thy dear name we raise'**
*Evening hymns are not sung as often now but they
contain prayerful words which are most helpful for
people at home. Here is an evening prayer which can
express the feelings of many of us as individuals, even
though it is written for the Church community as a
whole.*

652: **'God! When human bonds are broken'**
*There are not many hymns which speak directly to
situations where relationships are broken. Fred Kaan's
hymn is most helpful. It has a positive message of new
beginnings.*

653: **'We cannot measure how you heal'**
*Another thoughtful hymn about human suffering and
the need for healing. John Bell and Graham Maule have
found words fitting for the present day in this fine hymn.
Since it is set to the tune 'Angelus' there is a strong
reminder of the evening hymn: 'At even, when the sun
was set', a hymn on the same theme which was helpful
to a previous generation.*

This completes the selection of hymns for personal
devotional use. In addition we cannot neglect the
Psalms and Canticles many of which were written out
of personal experiences akin to our own. They will
continue to be a splendid resource for us all.

Passport Control

If you have worked your way through this book you will now be well and truly acquainted with *'Rejoice and Sing'*. Congratulations. If there is to be a 'Last Word' then it ought to be a reminder about your Passport.

A Passport serves at least two functions: it is a means of identity and it is an authorisation to cross frontiers.

It is a proof of identity. The fact that it is your face on it is important. Anything you have discovered or are about to discover must be related to you and your own situation. This book has helped you see the possibilities but only you can make them work or see that they are adapted to your circumstances. We all know that hymns are an emotive issue. It is hard to please some of the people some of the time, never mind all of the people all of the time!

It allows you the privilege of crossing boundaries. You are guests in a foreign country So be careful as you travel. Be appreciative of people's skills and creativity. Value words, cherish poetry, never lose your wonder or delight in music. Remember these things and it will be easier to carry others with you and to help them live in a strange land.

If you have a full Passport, it will be for ten years. You will then need a new photograph and you will look ten years older. This unpalatable thought reminds us that hymnbooks don't last for ever. *'Rejoice and Sing'* is already nearly five years old so it is not new any more. One day it will be replaced by another model. This book will then be redundant also.

When that time comes it will be hoped that some of the lessons you have learnt on the journey will still remain with you, and that you will be better equipped to travel to new places, with songs of praise upon your lips.